goingHOME

goingHOME

Facing Life's Final
Moments Without Fear

BILL KEMP | DIANE KERNER ARNETT

Kregel
Publications

Going Home: Facing Life's Final Moments Without Fear

Published by Kregel Publications, a division of Kregel, Inc., P.O. Box 2607, Grand Rapids, MI 49501.

Cover design: John M. Lucas

Library of Congress Cataloging-in-Publication Data
Kemp, Bill.
    Going home: facing life's final moments without fear / by Bill Kemp and Diane Kerner Arnett.
        p.   cm.
      1. Death—Religious aspects—Christianity. I. Arnett, Diane Kerner. II. Title.
BT825.K46 2005
236'.1—dc22   2004027792

ISBN 0-8254-2984-6

Printed in the United States of America

05 06 07 08 09 / 5 4 3 2 1

CONTENTS

Part 2: The People Around Us

We are not entirely present to ourselves
until the day of our death.

—Louis Lavelle
Christian philosopher, 1883–1951

LIFE IN THE PRESENT

Until now, we have worried about tomorrow—unpaid bills and upcoming appointments. The future has driven the present moment from our awareness. We have grown accustomed to knowing more about what is in the refrigerator than about what is in our hearts.

Then we hear a doctor say our days are numbered. Living for tomorrow doesn't have the urgency it once did. For us, life is now—this present moment. It is not a journey into the future, for tomorrow we will be going Home, with a capital *H*. Being a Christian gives us a right to use the word *home* to refer to two different places: the house where we currently keep our knickknacks, and the other home which Paul refers to as, "a building from God, an eternal house in heaven, not built by human hands" (2 Cor. 5:1).

When we begin to understand for ourselves that the time we may have upon this earth is short, we round a corner and enter a narrow passage. The future and the past are now other rooms, places in which we no longer dwell. We are not yet dead. We are not fully among the living, either. We are in the hallway in between.

Now we have certain decisions to make, affairs to put in order. But on the whole, we may feel out of control. People may ignore us or leave us to feel lonely. They may not be willing to take our wishes seriously. We may be struggling to resolve long-time conflicts. We want to use this time to make peace and prepare our souls and our legacies. It is hard to do that when people become distant. They are not in this hallway with us. How can they understand?

Even God may seem distant at this time, although we are heading to be with him. Take this to heart: there is nothing wrong with your faith. Just as your eyes need to adjust when they enter a darkened corridor, so also your eyes of faith are adjusting to the new experience of being in this passageway between earth and heaven.

Going Home aims to be your companion for this time of transition. Though we have glimpsed this hallway, we are not there with you. But we have sat with and listened to others who traveled Home slowly enough to share with us the things that encouraged them. This book is a tribute to the faith that kept them on their way.

Others have asked your questions and felt the same emotions that you feel. It is part of the journey. The journey toward death tests our courage. While wrestling with the deepest spiritual concerns of all mankind, we are also contending with pain, fatigue, medical treatments, loss of memory, and, often, new financial woes.

Through it all, we have a loving God who has promised not to abandon us. Keeping that promise close to our hearts will keep us steady through all the decisions, through all the afflictions, through all the lonely hours, until we reach the heavenly Home that has been promised us.

And when we get to the place Jesus himself prepared for us, we will find it is the place we have been homesick for all our lives, even though we didn't know it.

Part 1

A FEW THOUGHTS FOR THE JOURNEY

How should we live, and how do we keep our spiritual life on track during these final days?

And so we will be with the Lord forever.

—1 Thessalonians 4:17

Chapter 1

OUR OTHER HOME

"Is There Really Room in Heaven for Me?"

Many of our Lord's most cherished words and deeds come from the days right before he died. While in the passageway between earth and heaven, he prepared a plan for how and where he would die. He said good-bye to his friends and gave them a meaningful legacy. He fortified himself with prayer and the companionship of fellow Christians. Remember how on the night he was betrayed he urged his disciples to be near him in the garden as he prepared to suffer the next day with dignity? As he was crucified, he even shared his own experience of death by inviting a thief to receive salvation and enter into eternal life.

Mindful of those, like us, who would enter this passage after him, Jesus gave us a model for how we should act. He wanted us to have faith, to discharge our duties honorably, and to have no fear.

Wherever you are on the journey between this life and eternal life, Jesus is ahead of you. During the last meal he shared with his disciples, the fact of his death was real, yet he comforted them:

> Do not let your hearts be troubled. Trust in God; trust also in me. In my Father's house are many rooms; if it

were not so, I would have told you. I am going there
to prepare a place for you. And if I go and prepare a
place for you, I will come back and take you to be with
me that you also may be where I am. You know the
way to the place where I am going. (John 14:1–4)

With these words he said, "Look, you wait here. I'm going
to go ahead and make reservations."

The phrase *many rooms,* or in the King James translation of
the Bible, *many mansions,* means infinite space, a comfort to
those who are afraid they might not get in. We have all been
in those situations. Maybe we made plans but found we
couldn't get tickets or transportation or lodging. What if
heaven were like that? What if there were only room for 144,000
people? If you happen to be 144,001, you are out of luck. We
could live our lives as Christians only to meet Saint Peter and
hear him say, "Sorry, we're full."

But that is not what we are promised. Jesus says, *"I go and
prepare a place for you."* There is a place prepared for you! We
are meant to hold onto these words like a reserved seating
ticket. We have confirmation in hand; no one can bump us
from glory.

There is also an implied promise of individualized attention.
Jesus is preparing a place *especially* for you, and no one knows
you better than he does. Let your human imagination roam a
bit, and think about what your space in heaven would look
like. A cabin? An apartment? Would you have a certain favorite
chair? Would a window look out on a forest or waterfall? Would
you want to hear the sound of the sea or of thunder over the
mountains? What photos would be on the wall? What books
on the shelf? Is there something about that room that would
instantly tell you that Jesus had chosen it just for you?

Jesus is saying that our personal relationship with him is central. As long as we have accepted him into our hearts, there is nothing more that we need to do during our final weeks upon this earth to improve our chances of getting into heaven. We shouldn't look upon this time as a period in which we cram for life's final exam.

Jesus says it as simply as he can for the disciples: "Ye believe in God, believe also in me" (John 14:1 KJV).

To believe means to trust in the fact that you know Jesus, and he knows you. The disciples were not geniuses being asked to make some kind of great philosophical leap in order to be worthy of a room in eternity. Jesus simply asked them to hold onto their friendship with him. Later, in this same place, Jesus says: "I am the way and the truth and the life. No one comes to the Father except through me" (John 14:6).

What comfort! Jesus says that he, personally, is the way. Even with a map and directions a driver can get lost going someplace new. If Jesus had merely drawn a map to heaven for us or given us complicated teaching about salvation, then most of us would be lost. Instead, he is the friend from the place where you need to go; he offers to come with you and sits in the seat beside you, guiding you as you drive into the unknown.

By his presence, he is for you the way. When you need to cross over from here to heaven, Jesus promises to meet you and to be your way, your truth, your life. The same promise is also given in the Old Testament, when the Shepherd's Psalm says, "Yea, though I walk through the valley of the shadow of death, I will fear no evil: for thou art with me; thy rod and thy staff they comfort me" (Ps. 23:4 KJV).

I do believe; help me overcome my unbelief!

—Mark 9:24

Chapter 2

DEALING WITH DOUBTS

Having Doubts Doesn't Mean that Our Faith Is Weak

I llness means spending time alone with our thoughts. We wake at strange times or can't sleep at night. There are long, dark hours when few are at hand to keep us company. We think while we go through tests and treatments. Inevitably, we think—of times past, of people we hurt or failed to help. We remember responsibilities we shirked, people we made fun of. Fatigue and weakness can make our thoughts bleak— even drive us to despair.

As Christians, we may also deal with doubts about our own salvation, about God's mercy and love, about whether we will go to heaven. After all, we could have done better, couldn't we? We could have been a better parent, spouse, or friend. "Certainly," our mind nags, "I could have been a better Christian."

But God, who made each of us, knows we are weak and knows we will have doubts. Over and over in Scripture he tells of other imperfect people who committed even greater sins than ours but who loved God and were redeemed.

Parent? Don't take lessons from King David whose own children tried to kill him. Yet David was the apple of God's eye (Ps. 17:8).

Spouse? Even Solomon, the wisest person who ever lived, lacked wisdom in marriage.

Friend? The disciples could not keep awake with Jesus in Gethsemane.

Again and again, God tells us of his love for us in spite of our weaknesses. He remembers our sin no more.

Remember the story of the man who asked Jesus to heal his son? This man had taken the boy who suffered seizures and muteness since childhood to Jesus' disciples, and they had been unable to help. As he watched them fail, he was filled with doubts whether anyone could cure the boy. He turned to Jesus and asked:

> "But if you can do anything, take pity on us and help us."
> "'If you can'?" said Jesus. "Everything is possible for him who believes."
> Immediately the boy's father exclaimed, "I do believe; help me overcome my unbelief!" (Mark 9:22–24)

What did Jesus say to this wavering believer? Did he tell the sorrowful father to come back when he was sure? Did Jesus say that since the man was not one hundred percent certain, the boy would not be one hundred percent cured? No, Jesus cast out the spirit, took the boy by the hand, and lifted him up—completely, totally healed.

So if we, like the father here, believe but struggle, it is enough to tell God that. He already knows. Doubt cannot separate us from his love. Paul tells us:

> For I am convinced that neither death nor life, neither angels nor demons, neither the present nor the future, nor any powers, neither height nor depth, nor anything else in all creation, will be able to separate us from the love of God that is in Christ Jesus our Lord. (Romans 8:38–39)

Teach us to number our days aright,
that we may gain a heart of wisdom.

—Psalm 90:12

Chapter 3

"Is There Still Hope?"

*How Long Should We Hope when the Doctor
Keeps Giving Us Bad News?*

There are two dead ends of the human spirit. There are two places where we can become stuck in irrational thoughts—mired in self-pity and far from the "heart of wisdom," which God wants us to have.

The first is a condition named *denial*—the willful state in which we refuse to honor the information we have been given. A doctor gives us the results of our tests. Denial causes us to mistrust his interpretation, to ask for another, and then still another, opinion. Some people endure months of unnecessary prodding and expensive visits to specialists, all in vain attempts to change what cannot be changed, or at least will not be changed by denial.

Denial is only natural—a human response to the bare evidence of our own mortality. Our hearts need a moment to adjust to bad news. All people, when told they have a terminal illness, engage in some game of self-deception. Even very wise people have resorted to denying that they are sick at all. But to live in a state of denial too long sacrifices time we need for the important work of preparing for the world to come.

I (Bill) was called to the hospital late one night. An elderly man had suffered a serious heart attack and was in the intensive care unit. While he was not a churchgoer, his wife and daughter thought he might want to speak to a minister. We had a pleasant talk. I tried to steer him to spiritual things; he kept on talking about getting out in a few days. I knew his condition was much worse than he was letting on. I also knew that he was far from being right with God. The next day, he passed on.

God gives us grace for each moment. Sometimes we need to hear the bad news in order to receive the good news of Jesus' love and our eternal salvation. Even if we have been Christians for many years, there is still value to recognizing the wake-up call of our own mortality. We still need this time of preparation. Denial may rob us of the joys that come from receiving the grace God has for this moment.

There is a second dead end of the spirit. It is to abandon all hope of continued life on this earth. Even when painful, life is a gift from God. He sometimes deals us many more days than medical experts or our family expect. Sometimes we are too quick to believe bad news. Sometimes we lose hope too soon.

Consider the story of Lazarus in the gospel of John. Picture him gravely ill, drifting in and out of consciousness. The doctors give him no hope. All the test results confirm that, short of a miracle, he is going to die. So his family sends for a miracle—they beg Jesus to come. Only Jesus doesn't come. The days go by, Mary and Martha lose hope. They plan his funeral, make sure that his grave is prepared. True to predictions, Lazarus dies.

Three days later his miracle arrives—Jesus calls him forth from the grave and gives him total physical healing. As believers, we know that our God may also choose to do a physical miracle of total healing in our situation. He is still as active in the church today as he was for Lazarus, and there are many people who can testify to having recovered at death's doorstep. But things are always in God's hands, and faith teaches us that physical healing in this world is not the greatest gift that God may desire to give us.

Continuing to hope for our healing is very different from denying we are ill. Hope receives bad news and checks to see if there is a faithful and reasonable response to what others are telling us. Perhaps we should consider our funeral arrangements or estates. We can do that and still have hope. Perhaps we should tell our family the results of our most recent test. We can share bad news and still have hope. Hope is not based upon denying reality but rather upon affirming God's sovereignty. God may give us the miracle of an unexpected healing, or God may give us the miracle of a prepared and peaceful passing into his kingdom. Hope is required for both. When it comes to life on this earth, we believers should be the last to lose hope.

Even though Jesus raised him from the grave, Lazarus eventually died. Barring the return of our Lord, death is inevitable for each of us. The faith-affirming preparations that we make now for our eventual leaving this life will be useful at some point. This practical attitude complements our Christian hope; it affirms our faith that life is a gift.

The miraculous healing of Lazarus caused great rejoicing. It also prepared people to receive the greater miracle of Jesus' death and resurrection. Whether we live or we die, we should constantly point to the power of God. We should rejoice with those around us for every little miracle during this period of our life. If we have a good day or an encouraging report we should praise the Lord. Sharing these simple joys with others is important. By freeing ourselves from denial, we accept that we may lose the war against the disease that currently afflicts us. But in the battle for each day, there will be signs of God's grace and love. Hope enables us to recognize these "God moments." Hope lives even when the body is dying. By sharing that hope we become effective witnesses up to and beyond our last breath.

I have learned the secret of being content in any and every situation, whether well fed or hungry, whether living in plenty or in want. I can do everything through him who gives me strength.

—Philippians 4:12–13

Chapter 4

MAKING CHOICES KEEPS US IN THE GAME

No Matter the Circumstances,
We Still Have the Ability to Make Choices

When we know our final earthly hours are near, we have choices to make. Jesus did too. And when we balk at suffering and dying, what comfort to know that Jesus did too.

First, he chose to spend his final hours with friends at the Last Supper. There, he told them of his love and promised them a future. With him, they went to the Garden of Gethsemane. He asked them to keep watch as he prayed to our Father.

Then, Mark writes:

> Going a little farther, he fell to the ground and prayed that if possible the hour might pass from him. "*Abba, Father,*" he said, "everything is possible for you. Take this cup from me. Yet not what I will, but what you will." (Mark 14:35–36)

If we really believe that God knows best, shouldn't we just simply accept the fate we see before us? God does know best, but even his own son asked to be spared pain and death. In fact, Mark tells us that Jesus prayed that prayer twice. So there is no shame or sin in asking God to spare us.

Jesus asked to be spared but chose to offer obedience if death on the cross was God's plan. That is also a choice we each make—to accept God's answer whatever form it takes, whether healing or death.

Jesus made other choices in those last hours, too, just as we must. Certainly he could have told his disciples to go away and leave him alone, but he asked them to stay with him. He could have chosen not to eat or drink, but he ate a ritual feast. He could have said his time was up and done nothing, but he chose to care for other people until his last breath, even healing the soldier whose ear Peter cut off during the arrest in the garden. He did not berate the disciples for falling asleep; he prayed for them. While hanging on the cross, he made sure his mother would be cared for after his death. He assured the thief on the cross next to him that he would be with him that day in paradise. And he asked our Father to forgive the ones who crucified him.

Jesus could have made other choices. Who would have wondered at his fasting, praying, and being alone to prepare for his crucifixion? Who would have blamed him if he chose to remain totally mute and passive, knowing he had only hours to live?

So Jesus shows us clearly how to choose to live until the moment of our death. Can we think? We can pray. Can we feel? We can love and forgive. Can we taste? We can eat and drink. Do we have family obligations? We can make arrangements.

While we cannot choose the journey, we can choose how we will travel. One cancer patient I (Diane) shared a ward room with had been there for months. Her home was hundreds of miles away, and no one, not even her husband, could afford to stay with her any length of time. But Terry chose not to complain. Instead, she made her life there in the ward. Cards, posters, balloons, and photos adorned her walls. She got to know the staff and ran around the hospital as much as she was permitted. Eventually, Terry left the hospital. To this day, I don't know whether she overcame the disease, but I know that until the moment she died, she was most definitely living her life intentionally.

Then there was Janet. She had lots of family visit every day, but when they came she simply lay in her bed, moaning. What her family didn't know was that after they left, she would usually turn on her television loud enough for all four of us to hear and keep it on long after lights out. She would complain loud and long and ring for the nurses constantly. I would like to say that routine changed eventually, but it did not. And that is the way she behaved until she died.

Some people choose to play the invalid even when they are capable of more. No matter what circumstance, there are choices to be made.

Are you receiving medical care? You choose to do that. While you are receiving care, you choose how to behave as well—how to treat others, how to think of yourself, how to spend your time.

Those are big choices. Other choices, though small, can help you feel good. In my months in the hospital, I found the shuffle-shuffle sound that slippers made depressing. So I wore flip-flops instead—their clip-clap felt lively and purposeful, as though I were marching forward, not just keeping time.

Yes, drugs, pain, and exhaustion affect our behavior, but exercising choices and having some form of control can aid in keeping us from feeling helpless.

Planning for our loved ones' futures, writing our will, spending time in simple things like eating meals with friends— all can make the journey less painful.

As Christ did, we can find strength in choosing to stay in touch with our Father. He promises to give us strength for the day, for the moment to moment of living that is all any of us truly has.

The L ORD *himself goes before you and will be with you; he will never leave you nor forsake you. Do not be afraid; do not be discouraged.*

—Deuteronomy 31:8

Chapter 5

EXPECT LONELINESS

How Can We Deal with Loneliness?

When we are ill, so much of our time is spent waiting— waiting for the doctors, waiting for the nurse, waiting for daybreak. And while we wait, we can feel very lonely, despite seemingly being surrounded by people taking care of us.

Sometimes things we used to enjoy doing seem trivial now. Our body may be there, watching, but our minds are far away. Empathy and compassion can be difficult to achieve—I (Diane) remember one acquaintance going on and on about the pain of her ingrown toenail when I was months into treatment for the first cancer I had. I could neither escape her nor ignore her because we were with a group at a racetrack. Part of me wanted to scream at her: "Shut up, shut up, shut up! If it hurts that bad, cut it off! You'll still live! I'll trade places with you right now!"

Of course I didn't do that because serious illness sometimes brings unexpected tolerance for others, too. And it can also make us feel alone even when we are with a crowd.

They can't know what we're feeling. They haven't been there. And their particular illnesses can loom as large in their lives as our illness does in ours. But I've never forgotten the incident, either.

In surveys of people with terminal cancers, patients have said they fear isolation and abandonment above everything else. A study showed that patients dying in hospitals spent much of their last days alone. Nurses averaged forty-five visits daily, at two minutes per visit. Doctors averaged three visits of three minutes each. Family member visits averaged twenty-four minutes a day. All told, that still left patients with twenty-one hours and fifty-seven minutes to spend alone.[1] Even discounting time spent sleeping, that left many more hours alone than not.

In the hours before his death, Christ also longed for companionship, so he asked his disciples to watch with him in the garden while he prayed. He knows loneliness, and maybe that is why he promised: "And surely I am with you always, to the very end of the age" (Matt. 28:20).

It can be difficult to remember that, but it is true. We can call out to Christ at any time of day or night—we can tell him everything in our hearts and minds. Sometimes, while lying in a hospital bed or shuffled to the side of a hospital corridor awaiting tests, I would try to picture Jesus there with me. In my mind, we didn't talk, but he would be next to me, keeping watch with me. That exercise alone brought comfort because it took me from the knowledge that God is with us everywhere to some kind of feeling him there.

We can fight loneliness other ways, too. We can reach out—we can ask people to visit us or write to us or phone us. Some of the people we most want to spend time with are just those same considerate folks who worry about imposing on us or tiring us out. We only have to let them know it's all right. One friend and I would occasionally "play normal" by going shopping or going out to eat or just taking a drive. The ground rules were established that no matter what we were doing, if I felt ill or tired, she would bring me home. Except for that, we would not discuss the illness.

One good friend was only a few days from death when a group of us visited her at her home. We were all close friends, used to seeing each other every week at Bible study for eight years. That included the two years since her diagnosis, yet this was the first time she was not completely in her right mind. Lying in a hospital bed in her living room, she grinned when she saw us and said: "I don't know who you are or why you came, but I am glad you did."

Even with all the knowledge that God is with us, even with concerned friends and family, there will still be times when we feel lonely—but we will learn that is not the same as being alone and that as believers we are never truly alone. As David asked God in Psalm 139:7–8:

> Where can I go from your Spirit?
> Where can I flee from your presence?
> If I go up to the heavens, you are there;
>   if I make my bed in the depths, you are there.

In Christ we have what Proverbs 18:24 calls "a friend who sticks closer than a brother." And when we see him face to face, we will never feel lonely again.

For just as the sufferings of Christ flow over into our lives, so also through Christ our comfort overflows.

—2 Corinthians 1:5

Chapter 6

"It Hurts"

How Can We Deal with Pain?

P ain is not the worst thing that happens to us in life, but it is the thing that gets our attention. In fact, that is pain's job. When God designed the human body, he crafted our nervous system with great care. Not only do the nerves in our hands warn us when things are too hot to hold, they also speak in a way that overrides all other concerns, so that protecting our body comes first. Our minds may be focused on cooking a meal, but pain ensures that we will drop a hot pot rather than endanger a limb.

This God-designed ability of pain to get our attention is true of emotional and spiritual hurts as well. Pain ensures that the soul is not ignored. Whether it is physical or emotional, pain is an inevitable part of the final stage of life's journey. At some point we have to face our pain squarely and decide what to do about it. Pain is not designed to be ignored.

Unfortunately, one of the cruel ironies of illness is that pain often persists in situations where we can do nothing more to help the root cause. Like the fire klaxon that keeps howling even though all the firemen are present and fighting the blaze, so pain sometimes overstays its welcome. Sometimes people will ask, "Is it all right for Christians to take drugs for pain?" My response is, "Is it all right to turn off the fire alarm once everyone has been warned?" If the problem is physical pain, then modern medications are a blessing in that they can help alleviate some of pain's overzealousness. Properly used, they can stretch out the number of good days that we have. Further, if medications are used as prescribed, addiction rarely occurs. And if you are terminally ill, why feel guilty about depending on drugs?

If the pain that we are experiencing is related to emotional issues or broken relationships, then that needs to be addressed as well. Pain always exists for a purpose. Sometimes it prompts us to set pride aside and seek reconciliation and forgiveness. Sometimes it causes us to deal more honestly with God. Often it makes us gentler and more compassionate people. As we recognize and deal with our own pain, we become channels for God's grace to other people.

The apostle Paul writes,

> Praise be to the God and Father of our Lord Jesus Christ, the Father of compassion and the God of all comfort, who comforts us in all our troubles, so that we can comfort those in any trouble with the comfort we ourselves have received from God. (2 Corinthians 1:3–4)

When we are diagnosed with a terminal condition, we may feel that there is little that we can do about our illness, but we will still have many choices about pain and our lifestyle. Often medical staff or others can give us good advice about how to take charge of our pain. If our pain is cyclical, that is, always becoming more intense at a certain time of day, we may want to time our medications differently or plan our activities around this understanding. We also may want to pay close attention to how medication affects our being present for those we want to see. The point is to make informed choices, because choices keep us in the game rather than sidelined by pain or sleep.

When my wife and I were expecting our first child, we attended Lamaze natural childbirth classes. We were aware that reducing the amount of drugs used during the delivery was good for the baby. While my wife's labor wasn't entirely pain-free, the experience made us aware that choices could be made about pain and that some tools can be learned to enable us to be more comfortable in stressful situations.

Moving from this world to the next is very much like childbirth. The pains that we experience are both physical and emotional. For the Christian, joy and hope overcome the fear and pain associated with both childbirth and death. But in the moment-to-moment struggle we need support and help to keep the goal in sight.

The first thing we learned in Lamaze was to pair up with a dependable coach. The father or some other designated "coach" would study natural childbirth alongside the mother. He would be a committed companion and encourager, reducing the anxiety of delivery, hopefully reducing its pain. In facing terminal illness, we also have to seek out people who will be the right kind of coaches for us. There are those who will accept our illness and support us, making us less fearful. In reducing our fears, they reduce our pain.

It is important that the people around us accept that we will have some good days and some bad days. It is not helpful to us when people expect us to always be cheerful. It also doesn't help us when people tell us that our pain is not as bad as we think. Our pain is our pain. A good coach will respect our pain but also lift our focus toward the goal of living the remaining days that the Lord gives us with dignity. A good coach will pray with us when we ask and for us when we feel too blue to pray for ourselves.

Lamaze class also introduced us to the concept that certain breathing techniques can reduce the anxiety that accentuates the body's pain response. Focusing on breathing slowly in and out from the diaphragm (the area closest to our belly) reduces the tension in our muscles and can cause our minds to detach from the experience of pain. Adding to this a remembrance of a favorite place or a peaceful moment elevates our awareness away from where our anxiety dwells. Many people find this helpful when they have to face an uncomfortable medical test or endure treatments.

Along this same line, some Christians incorporate simple prayers into the way they respond to stress. I, personally, have often used the line from Psalm 23, "He restoreth my soul . . ." (v. 3 KJV), as a one-line prayer when I have to face distressing occasions. I repeat it over in my head, each time I breathe, until I am calm and focused on his promises rather than my fears.

So pain is not the worst thing that we face in this life. What we do with and about pain is our choice. Sometimes it helps to remind ourselves that God knows our pain and experienced the fullness of suffering through Christ on the cross. Other times we must take the initiative to request and use the best modern medicine can offer us. Through it all, we need to expand our dependence upon the prayers and support of others as well as our own spiritual resources. We are not alone; the God of all comfort is with us.

*Who of you by worrying can add a
single hour to his life? . . . Therefore do not
worry about tomorrow, for tomorrow will
worry about itself. Each day has enough
trouble of its own.*

—Matthew 6:27, 34

Chapter 7

REASONABLE FEARS

*How Can We Find Peace of Mind and Heart
in the Face of Our Fears?*

When we are sick, it's easier than usual to be afraid. Even as believers, we may fear so many things even if we do not fear death itself.

For our physical bodies, we fear fatigue, pain and suffering, side effects from treatment, or the idea of depending on others to feed and bathe us. Emotionally, we fear abandonment, helplessness, and despair. Mentally, we fear confusion and forgetfulness. Spiritually, we may even fear judgment, despite knowing that Christ has washed us clean in God's eyes. In all these ways, we may also fear the unknown, and dying is the unknown.

Feeling fear does not mean we lack faith—it only means we are human. Fear is understandable and even reasonable. It can prompt us to be cautious about things.

If we fear that sharing our estate will cause friction among loved ones, we can make a will or give away belongings before we die. If we fear that we may lose the ability to speak for ourselves later, we can make our wishes known now. It is reasonable to wonder what will become of our families, our homes, our pets, and our belongings. It is reasonable to worry about side effects of a new treatment or medication.

When fear rocks out of control to become terror, then it is unreasonable and unhealthy. Terror can paralyze us, making us unable to think, to sleep, to eat—to function at all. Many of us have had the experience of leaving on vacation. A little way down the road, we begin second-guessing our preparations in our minds. Suddenly, we may think we left the coffee pot on. We don't remember turning it off, but that is so routine we probably wouldn't remember it.

Now what do we do with this fear? We may ask our spouse if she noticed the coffee pot was on. We may phone a neighbor or whoever is looking after our house while we are gone to double-check the coffee pot for us. If we are just pulling out of the driveway, we may even stop and go back inside the house to check the pot for ourselves. These are all reasonable responses to a reasonable fear that leaving the coffee pot on might cause a fire while we are gone.

We could respond in terror. We could delay our journey for hours just to make certain for ourselves that the coffee pot is off. If we are particularly afraid, we might check and double-check and triple-check and quadruple-check the coffee pot. In the extreme, we could cancel our vacation and never leave the house again, ever, because the coffee pot might be left on, and we just know the house will indeed burn down.

One difference between responses of fear and responses of terror is this: trusting someone. If our spouse says she turned off the coffee pot or saw it being done, we trust her witness. If a caretaker says he will go check the coffee pot right away and turn it off, we trust him to do so. If we do not trust someone else, then we find ourselves responding in terror, able only to cope with things we think we can control.

So faith is the remedy for fear. If we trust God to take care of things, we can rest easy. When we feel fear, we just need to appeal to him, our steadfast and dependable Creator. How he handles things is up to him; as the saying goes, "Sometimes he calms the storm, and sometimes he calms the sailor."

We can't always understand the calm, but we know when it comes. Before he died, Jesus told his disciples and us:

> Peace I leave with you; my peace I give you. I do not give to you as the world gives. Do not let your hearts be troubled and do not be afraid. (John 14:27)

Bear with each other and forgive whatever grievances you may have against one another. Forgive as the Lord forgave you.

—Colossians 3:13

Chapter 8

FORGIVEN AND FORGIVING

How Can We Forgive Others? How Can We Forgive Ourselves?

I n my city (Bill) there is an ambulance-chasing lawyer who appears on TV seeking to represent people who feel that they have been wronged in some way. He begins his ads by saying that if you have been injured in an accident or have been the victim of some form of malpractice, you need to see a lawyer, preferably him. There are big settlements to be awarded to you for your pain and suffering. He ends each advertisement with the words, "Get what's coming to you!" His ads are a sign of the times. It seems that everyone today insists on getting what's coming to him or her.

I think that much of Jesus' life and ministry moved in the opposite direction. Instead of insisting on the honor he deserved as the Son of God, he "made himself nothing, taking the very nature of a servant" (Phil. 2:7). Instead of giving prostitutes and tax collectors the judgment and hostility his society felt that they deserved for their sins, he became a friend of sinners (Matt. 11:19). Instead of teaching people how to get even, he taught them how to turn the other cheek (Matt. 5:39). Once when asked to arbitrate between two brothers who were arguing over an inheritance, Jesus refused to even listen to the case (Luke 12:13–21). He had seen too many relationships soured by greed. Getting what we think we deserve rarely makes us content and certainly does not heal our souls.

We all carry a mental list of the things we think that we deserve. We remember when people fail to give us what they promised. We may be resentful about a promotion we didn't receive, an inheritance that went to someone else, or an honor that bypassed us. We may add to our list the friends who betrayed us, the children who neglected us, or the spouse who was unfaithful. Whether it is long or has just a few special bad eggs—this list itself is deadly. As we approach our graduation to heaven above, it is a burden we can no longer cart around. Forgiveness is a matter of losing the list to gain our souls.

The truth is that none of us can afford to get what is coming to us. The apostle Paul says with unerring honesty that "there is no one righteous, not even one" (Rom. 3:10). We all fall short of God's standard of holiness (Rom. 3:23). If we were to get what was coming to us, it wouldn't be heaven. Even the best lawyer on earth cannot sway the judge who sees the very intentions of our hearts. For even the best of people, heaven is a gift, not earned, but freely given because of the forgiveness which is ours in Christ.

We are forgiven because:

> God so loved the world that he gave his one and only Son, that whoever believes in him shall not perish but have eternal life. (John 3:16)

What God has done is laid down another truth, one that is at cross-purposes to the rule that all people should get what they deserve. When we accept Christ we receive for ourselves complete and total forgiveness. We will not get what is coming to us when we stand before the judgment throne. Instead, we will get the heaven that Christ has opened for us by his sacrifice on the cross.

It may well be that God has given you this time for you to do your part of the critical work of forgiveness. The time that stretches from when you receive the diagnosis of a terminal illness until when you leave this earth belongs in part to three special acts of forgiveness that you are called to participate in.

First, you must forgive yourself. When you became a Christian, God gave to you complete and total forgiveness. The message of Psalm 103:12, "as far as the east is from the west, so far has he removed our transgressions from us," is true for all of your sins. God refuses now to be reminded of your past failures. We, however, often continue to nag ourselves about the things God has removed from us. The work of God's forgiveness is completed when we forgive ourselves.

Completing the work of God's forgiveness may involve restitution. If we can in some way make amends to a person we have wronged, we should do that. Jesus says,

> If you are offering your gift at the altar and there remember that your brother has something against you, leave your gift there in front of the altar. First go and be reconciled to your brother; then come and offer your gift. (Matt. 5:23–24)

As Christians, our deaths are an act of sacred worship in that moment we place the gift of our lives upon God's altar. Finding the humility to seek the forgiveness of others may be an important preparation for that worship. If the person we have wronged is no longer living, we may wish to make a gift in his or her honor to a charity he or she would have supported.

The important thing is that we find closure in our own hearts about our past failures. The people we have wronged may not always be able to tell us that they forgive us, but we need to forgive ourselves.

Along this same line, you also need to forgive other people. As Thomas Fuller puts it, "He who cannot forgive others breaks the bridge over which he must pass himself."[1] You may say to yourself, "Well, I would forgive her if she were sorry," or, "It's up to him to make the first move." But, at this stage in your life, you cannot afford to wait for others to act in such a way as to deserve your forgiveness. It's not about giving people what they deserve; it's about giving them what Christ would give them. Forgiveness, like love, needs to be unconditional.

Sometimes people will say that they can't forgive, but God does not ask us to do anything that is beyond us. The truth is that you are in need of the spiritual healing which will come to you when you truly forgive those who have angered you. In the end, it's not about them; it is about you. You cannot pass peacefully into the next world burdened by bitterness. So you must forgive them as Christ has forgiven you.

Finally, you may also need to forgive God. It is only natural to get angry at him for the illness that limits your mobility and will someday take your life. Many people express hostility toward their doctor, the medical staff, and their families, when the real object of their anger is God. Ultimately, he is the one to blame. You may be reluctant to admit that you feel this way.

The book of Job reminds us of several important facts:

- A person can be angry at God and still be a person of faith.
- God has pretty big shoulders; he doesn't blame us for the way that we feel.

- God is mysterious, and much of his plan is hidden from us.
- Even patient people like Job get frustrated because they cannot understand why God allows certain things to happen.
- God is still God, and one day we will understand.

Everyone has regrets. All people harbor dark thoughts of things they wish had turned out differently. Some people wish for children that they never were able to have or for a spouse that would have been a true soul mate. Others long for the ability to travel or remain on earth long enough to see their grandchildren. In forgiving God we accept the life that we have received. Life on this earth is not perfect, but it is filled with his grace. And when we leave this earth, our lives will stand complete. He will fold us into his arms, and he will dry every tear from our eyes, and Love will forgive all.

A cheerful heart is good medicine,
but a crushed spirit dries up the bones.

—Proverbs 17:22

Chapter 9

HAVING A MERRY HEART

Laughter Is Seriously Okay

Sometimes people think the first victim of your terminal diagnosis is your sense of humor. After all, dying is such serious business. When facing eternity and eternal judgment, how can you laugh?

You can laugh because God has made us that way—able to laugh at all parts of life—and dying is just another part of life. Certainly the Creator who designed the giraffe designed our funny bones as well.

Sometimes I (Diane) wish the shortest verse in the Bible were not "Jesus wept" but "Jesus laughed." How far that would go toward putting us at ease with the Savior! Yet while Scripture does not explicitly say Jesus laughed, we know that he was constantly making little jokes, playing with his friends. I think he must have laughed as well as he preached. (Aren't the best preachers the ones who can keep our attention with humor?)

One video series portrays the book of Matthew. In it, we see Jesus grinning and playing and teasing his friends and followers. The ending struck a real chord in me. After telling his disciples "And surely I will be with you always, to the very end of the age" the camera pulls back, and Jesus smiles a huge smile, beckoning to the camera to follow him.

I would like to follow him, I thought. Why, I could invite him in for coffee without fussing about my housekeeping, just like I do my best friend. It seems like it would just be fun to be with him.

Trying to maintain a sense of humor doesn't mean that we deny our illness. However, neither does it mean adopting a false "positive attitude." If all it required to be healed were a "positive attitude," no one would ever die. In fact, no matter how cheerful or hopeful, we do think about our approaching deaths, and we do want to take care of things before we go. How frustrating it is when we voice our very real concerns and are brushed off with commands to "be positive" instead of finding a sympathetic ear. It's important to find a way to communicate these wishes—no matter how slight. One man told me he offered to do anything for his dying friend; the friend said, "Okay—help me clean out my garage?" They did.

If a spouse or child cannot or will not hear our serious concerns, there must be someone we can confide in, with the understanding that our wishes will be communicated to our survivors on our death.

Humor, even gallows humor, keeps us balanced and involved in living. As a cancer patient, I often roomed with a seventy-something farmer named Inez. As she ate ice cream she had persuaded a doctor to prescribe for her from the cafeteria (despite her diabetes), together we watched Independence Day fireworks out our ward window. After my discharge, I would visit with Inez following my biweekly and monthly checkups.

One day when I went to the ward, the charge nurse told me that Inez was "not doing well." She wanted simply to die at home. I found her alone in the solarium in a mobile lounge chair with her IV running.

In the course of our visit, I mentioned seeing that a particular inexperienced nurse we both disliked was back on the floor and asked how she was treating her. Inez said, "Ha, very nice."

"Oh, she probably just wants you to put her in your will," I said.

"Fooled her," said Inez, "don't have a will." We said good-bye with hugs and kisses. I returned to my home a hundred miles away. Two or three days later, Inez also returned home and, as she wished, died the next day.

Another friend in the days before she died kept thinking she saw someone on the porch outside her window. Despite reassurances that no one was there, she still felt a presence. Sitting with her one time, I said, "So, okay, maybe you can see someone I can't. And if it's someone from heaven, at least let's hope it's Gregory Peck or Cary Grant." To that, my friend said, "It better be Gregory Peck; I never did like Cary Grant." And days later, that friend, too, died.

In our dying as in our living, we can choose our outlook, even if we can't choose the circumstances. We can choose who to spend time with, and how. We can wallow in unrelenting misery, or we can seek the grace—and humor—of the moment. I think Jesus would want us to laugh.

*Jesus Christ is the same yesterday
and today and forever.*

—Hebrews 13:8

Chapter 10

I F

If We Recover, What Then Is to Be Expected?

God, in his unchanging love and mercy, may heal you—even you. And if you are miraculously healed, you will face a strange situation. I (Diane) know. I did.

At first, you will likely promise yourself to appreciate every moment, to proclaim to the world what God has done. You may decide that he has called you to a special mission—and, of course, he has, but it may not be the mission you envision.

You see, God calls each of us to accomplish things which no one else can. He equips and strengthens us for our callings. And while some folks may be led to a new ministry, most of us will simply be asked to be more faithful in what we were doing before we got sick.

Did Jesus' friend Lazarus become the leader of the new church after his miraculous recovery? No, that was Peter's job; Lazarus appears to have gone on serving as he did before his illness. In the New Testament we see many instances of miraculous healings, but often the individual is not named then or ever mentioned again. There is no quicker way to drain the joy of our healing from our lives and ruin our testimony than to tell ourselves it is not enough for us to thank God and move on. Prideful guilt can cripple us.

We may ask, "Why did God heal me?" Until we see him

face to face we will likely never really know. Truth be told, it could be that who we are had nothing to do with our healing. It may be for us, as it was for the paralytic:

> Some men came, bringing to him a paralytic, carried by four of them. Since they could not get him to Jesus because of the crowd, they made an opening in the roof above Jesus and, after digging through it, lowered the mat the paralyzed man was lying on. When Jesus saw their faith, he said to the paralytic, "Son, your sins are forgiven. . . .
>
> "I tell you, get up, take your mat and go home." He got up, took his mat and walked out in full view of them all. (Mark 2:3–5, 11–12)

You see, Jesus commended the faith of the paralytic's friends. So it may be the faith of someone else who is praying for us whose prayers God answers. It might even be someone we don't know.

It could be for you as it was for the man blind since birth.

> His disciples asked him, "Rabbi, who sinned, this man or his parents, that he was born blind?"
>
> "Neither this man nor his parents sinned," said Jesus, "but this happened so that the work of God might be displayed in his life." (John 9:2–3)

Jesus healed the man who, when grilled by church leaders later about the who, how, and why of his healing, said: "One thing I do know. I was blind but now I see!" (John 9:25).

Being healed of a major illness may not make us eloquent preachers for God. And, of course, it could be for you an answer to your own prayer and faith, as it was for the woman who had been bleeding for years (Luke 8:43–48).

No matter the reason for our healing, in our recovery we may truly believe that we will experience this overwhelming gratitude and joy every minute of our restored lives. But we will not. And praise God that we cannot, for if God had endowed us with the ability to maintain our mountaintop highs, we could also continually relive the pain of our wilderness lows. It is a natural part of God's healing that we humans cannot live at the extremes of our emotions.

That does not mean we will forget, however. And there will be special times in our lives that we relive our experience with extreme gratitude. We will be more aware of God's goodness, but though we try, we cannot be constantly aware. It is enough that we are more easily reminded.

For similar reasons, we may find that what is a life-defining experience for us may be a bad memory our loved ones may not want to recall. We did fight for our lives, but if the experience pervades our every waking moment, it may be a sign that we need professional counsel.

Oddly enough, our recovery may cost us friendships—not because we drive people away, but because some people are attracted to unhappiness or difficulty. When the difficulty passes, they will, too. On the other hand, friends who drew apart during our illness may again draw near. We may or may not respond in kind.

Odder still, our dearest friends may choose not to believe our healing was a miracle, despite any evidence we show them. While they accept that we believe we experienced a miracle, they may not consider it such. There is not evidence enough in all the world to convince them—only the Spirit of God can do that.

If our illness resulted from a missed diagnosis or medical

carelessness, we may be tempted to try to right the wrong with a lawsuit or confrontation. God may indeed lead us to do those things, but more often it seems our compassionate Creator asks us to forgive and go on. Time, money, and emotions can be better spent in building than in destroying.

And as we continue living our "normal" lives, we may not be wiser or stronger for the experience. We may simply be restored—and isn't that enough?

Explaining God's command to do our jobs with all our might to his glory, the Rev. Martin Luther King Jr. once said: ". . . my friends, even if it falls your lot to be a street sweeper, go on out and sweep streets like Michelangelo painted pictures; sweep streets like Handel and Beethoven composed music; sweep streets like Shakespeare wrote poetry; (Go ahead) sweep streets so well that all the host of heaven and earth will have to pause and say, 'Here lived a great street sweeper who swept his job well.'"[1]

Even though we are healed like Lazarus, eventually we will die as Lazarus did. And so? As a priest once said at a funeral: "Each day of our life we walk with God. At the end of every day, we return to our own beds, until one day God says to us: 'Why don't you come home with me?'"

Amen. So be it.

Part 2

THE PEOPLE
AROUND US

*How do we strengthen and find strength
in our relationships with others?*

We have different gifts, according to the grace given us. . . . If it is serving, let him serve; . . . if it is encouraging, let him encourage; if it is contributing to the needs of others, let him give generously.

—Romans 12:6–8

Chapter 11

DIFFERENT STROKES FOR DIFFERENT FOLKS

How Do We Handle the Different Ways
People Respond to Our Illness?

When Morrie Schwartz was first diagnosed with ALS (Lou Gehrig's disease), his wife took on all the added responsibilities of his terminal condition. But as his disease progressed, she went back to work, and a variety of friends and family and home-care professionals were engaged to care for Morrie. Morrie could have complained and made his wife feel guilty, but he knew that she did not need to prove her love. Instead, he intentionally invited casual acquaintances and even strangers to experience some part of his life's final chapter. The most unexpected participant was a former student, Mitch Albom, who found himself stopping by on Tuesdays to act as confidant, biographer, and participant in Morrie's deathbed class on how to live a love-filled life all the way to the end. Because Morrie was sensitive to Mitch's skills and natural curiosity, the tale of Morrie's final year has become the inspirational book, *Tuesdays with Morrie*, which has given courage to thousands.[1]

Our attitude toward those who care for us can be one of clinging manipulation, or it can be one which frees us to receive the blessing behind Jesus' words:

> Give, and it will be given to you. A good measure, pressed down, shaken together and running over, will be poured into your lap. For with the measure you use, it will be measured to you. (Luke 6:38)

When we make it a point to be interested in each person we encounter, we keep ourselves from becoming a burden. Our disease may cause us to need more and more personal attention, but nothing keeps our spirits from giving more and more love. We can take an interest in the lives of the healthcare workers we encounter. We can choose to be encouraging and gracious to each person who enters our room. In doing this we make care giving a two-way street.

In relating with our family and friends, we need to be attuned to how each person is unique. Each has to deal with our illness; each has to deal with fears of losing us and what that means. We may be flustered when the person we most depend on chooses to return to work or to continue doing activities without us. Our minds may be aware of the financial burdens which require them to work, but we are still jealous of their time spent away. In our hearts it may take us a while to accept that they need to keep some part of their lives "normal." They are doing what is healthy for them and for us. Instead of insisting that they keep a bedside vigil, we need to support their spiritual and mental health. We need to accept the gift of time each person is able to give us.

People are honored when we tailor our requests to what they are able to give. One striking thing about Morrie Schwartz was his willingness to allow acquaintances and visitors to participate in his personal care. He chose not to allow shame over the effects of his disease interfere with his final chance to communicate with people. Our natural inclination when we lose the capacity to do things for ourselves is to feel embarrassed. This can sometimes lead to two unhealthy extremes in behavior—isolation or suffocation. We may shut close family and friends out of our lives because we don't want them to know details of our problems. We may impulsively shy away from letting people touch us. However, there are often people who want to help us, if only we are willing to let them.

Sometimes we do the opposite, clinging to loved ones but hesitating to make full use of the healthcare and social services available. Allowing strangers into our homes or hospital rooms to poke and prod us or to go over our finances often feels like a painful intrusion on our dignity and privacy. Sometimes figuring out insurance and financial regulations may overwhelm us with complications we don't feel up to facing, so we don't deal with them. We soon discover that isolating ourselves takes a high toll. The less respect we show others, the quicker they go away. Perhaps the nurses we wouldn't talk to choose to keep their visits with us as brief as possible. Perhaps the social worker we refused had ways to save our families money or time. Worst of all, our family feels burdened because we are thrusting cares on them which would be better handled by a healthcare professional or could be easily undertaken by willing friends.

Whether we are dealing with strangers or friends, it is important to recognize that each individual has limits. We also, however, need to be mindful that God has given these persons something to contribute which is an honor for them to give. There will be times when we are surprised by how willing people are to help us. They feel useful and appreciated because we have invited them to perform the service that God has given them the talent and desire to do. Other times we will sense that we have encountered the limit to someone's capacity to meet our need. The trick then is to thank her graciously for what she has given and prayerfully look to see who else God wishes to bring into our lives.

Jesus' death on the cross was a lesson in having the humility to depend upon others. Weak and frail, he allowed Simon of Cyrene to carry his cross. In poverty, he could not pay for his own grave, so he let Joseph loan him one. He thirsted but could not fetch his own water, so he accepted a drink from the strangers who were waiting for him to die. Even his family members were unable to take on his personal obligations, so he gave the care of his mother into the hands of his friend John. None of those who were expected to stay by him did, but he found other people to share his final hours, people God blessed for giving what they could give.

Some people will respond to your illness with utter denial. Others may act as if you are dead already. Take it all with a grain of salt—you yourself will have ups and downs as you try to figure out how you feel about your illness. Be aware that others are wrestling with their own feelings, too, whether or not they show it.

The less we pigeon-hole people with our expectations of them, the more we are able to let them simply walk this journey with us. This allows some people to give far more time and attention to us than we feel worthy of and others simply to still be our friends. It is a unique experience for all, and as each has been given, each will provide.

Then all the disciples deserted him and fled.

—Matthew 26:56

Chapter 12

DESERTERS AND FOUL-WEATHER FRIENDS

True Friends Sometimes Go, and False Friends Stay and Stay:
How Do We Know Whom to Trust?

I n these final days of our lives on earth, we may find that
friends we depend on desert us, just as the disciples deserted
Jesus when he was arrested in the Garden of Gethsemane. And
like Job, we may find "comforters" who cling to us and drain
our faith.

Through no fault of our own, the trial of our dying may
attract false friends and repel true friends. In Jesus' last hours,
Judas kissed him, and Peter not only deserted Christ like the
other disciples but also denied him three times. Yet we know
that Judas was a false friend, but Peter went on to show his
love for Jesus by leading his church.

Jesus reacted to the disciples' desertion with compassion
and forgiveness. When he first appeared to the disciples in
the upper room after his death, he did not say, "You disap-
point me, you ingrates. You betrayed me. You denied me. You
let me down." Instead, the first words he said were: "Peace be
with you!" (John 20:19).

And then, he said it again (see John 20:21).

Some people who really are true friends and good people
may desert us. They will have reasons that may not satisfy us

but need to be heard. Family members or close friends may have difficulty seeing us ill. They may wish to remember us as the strong, healthy person we were for them for so many years. Others may have a hard time entering a hospital or being around the smells associated with medical treatment. Just the idea of death may terrify some who will choose to hide from us rather than confront their own mortality. Realistic or not, people may fear catching our illness. Our suffering may be a painful reminder of someone else they loved and lost. Others will avoid us in order to help them deny the seriousness of our situation.

On the other hand, some people may be using our situation to satisfy their own neurotic needs. These are false friends, foul-weather friends. They hang around listening for bad news and delight in spreading it to the world. Some may try to influence us into giving them substantial inheritance for their own gain. Others may simply want to be in power over us. Hard as it may seem to believe, some just enjoy other people's misfortune.

In Jesus' life, fear for their own lives seems to have motivated the disciples to desert him. Further, the same fear probably led Peter to deny Christ without thinking. Scripture tells us that when the cock crowed, Peter realized what he had done and wept bitterly. When Judas betrayed Christ, his actions revealed his true motivations in being a disciple. Judas was treasurer for the group and was paid thirty pieces of silver for identifying Christ with a kiss. Maybe he only acted for money. Some believe that Judas did not truly believe Christ was the Messiah but jumped on the political bandwagon, hoping that Jesus' growing popularity would restore the Jews to ruling Israel. Judas wanted to be important, to be a winner. When the tide began to turn, he cut his losses.

Although we are not perfect like Christ, God has graciously given us examples of other mere humans reacting to deserters and foul-weather friends. Consider Naomi who was left a widow and childless after ten years in the land of Moab. Wedding ceremonies often include the pledge of her daughter-in-law, Ruth, to remain with her: "Where you go I will go" (Ruth 1:16). Not many recall Naomi's other daughter-in-law, Orpah, who reluctantly and in tears did as Naomi repeatedly urged and returned to her mother's home. Naomi had never intended for either daughter-in-law to remain with her and had even blessed them as she prepared to leave, assuming they would stay in Moab.

In these days, God willing, we will be blessed with at least one "Ruth" in our life. Probably, we will also have an Orpah or two. Did Orpah love her mother-in-law less than Ruth? We don't know and can't really say. Maybe she was more afraid of leaving her homeland for a strange culture and country than she could bear, even for love of Naomi. Naomi truly wanted the best for Orpah and accepted her decision.

If people leave us, it does not mean they do not love us anymore.

By the same token, people who come to us in our affliction may not be doing so out of love at all. Remember Job's three friends? They went to visit Job when he was sitting on an ash heap, covered in boils, financially ruined, and mourning that all his children had died. Each man told Job they knew why he was suffering so—God was punishing him for some "secret sin" and that to end his pain, Job only had to "get right with God." They were condemning and judging Job. And when God revealed the error of their thinking, he asked Job to do one thing—pray for them.

Even today, many well-meaning and deeply spiritual people

will tell us that we are suffering because of sin. And if, like Job, we protest that we know of no sin, they tell us that ignorance is no guarantee that we did not sin. In a way, they are perhaps trying to reassure themselves that if they continue to lead holy lives, tragedy will not befall them. That belief is not consistent with Scripture at all; God's only son led a perfect life, yet he was unjustly accused and murdered. Do we deserve better? Can we, through mere human effort, earn a happy ending? Of course not.

How do we respond to deserters and foul-weather friends? Like Naomi, if we love them we want them to be happy. Like Job, we pray for them and turn a deaf ear to their "help." In spite of our own hurt feelings, like Christ, we wish them peace.

> Be kind and compassionate to one another, forgiving each other, just as in Christ God forgave you. (Ephesians 4:32)

*There will be more rejoicing in heaven over one
sinner who repents than over ninety-nine
righteous persons who do not need to repent.*

—Luke 15:7

Chapter 13

WHAT ABOUT UNSAVED LOVED ONES?

*Is There Still Hope for Those Who Do Not
Share Our Love for Jesus?*

I n *The Adventures of Huckleberry Finn,* Miss Watson tries to
lure Huck into behaving better by telling him about the
wonders of heaven. To Huck the thought of doing nothing
but playing a harp all day sounds pretty awful, but before
leaving the subject, he asks her if she thinks Tom Sawyer will
make it into the good place. When she says, "Not by a consid-
erable sight," he decides not to try for glory either.

Like Huck, we may be less than enthusiastic about heaven
because we are afraid that it will separate us from someone
whom we care about. On the other hand, some of the people
we consider to be unsaved are choosing to remain outside the
fold because of loyalty to the gang they hang out with. We
may have a hard time judging how they really feel about the
Lord because their behavior is determined by the pack they
run with.

This is perhaps the point, since salvation is a matter of the
heart. It depends on faith and not outward deeds. God does
not grant any of us the ability to judge who is and who isn't
saved. We can look in our own heart and have assurance about
the faith relationship which saves us, but we cannot look into

the heart of another person. When and how an individual comes to this faith in Jesus is a mystery. In the end, we only know for sure about ourselves. Rather than dividing the world into saved and unsaved, we should think of people as being either assured of their salvation or still looking for it.

As we think about our non-Christian loved ones, perhaps we should keep in mind the story Jesus tells of a lost sheep. The shepherd loved even the lost one and, in the end, searched and found the sheep, rescuing her from certain death and bringing her home. We should not give up hope about anyone. Jesus reinforces this image of the lost being found by telling us about a prodigal son who finds his way home. The greater the distance a person has traveled from God, the more rejoicing when he turns and repents. We cannot rush anyone to that sacred decision but must trust that a person will make it when ready.

In the meantime we should think carefully about our witness toward her. Have we talked about our faith in language that she would understand? Are we careful not to be judgmental or to let our feelings about his lifestyle prevent us from showing Christ's love? Simply, our goal is to lead our loved ones to Jesus, not to get them to go to our church. We need to use the openings that the Holy Spirit gives us to speak about our personal faith and experience rather than to argue about religion.

How does our attitude about our illness affect our witness? When it comes to sharing faith, listeners find honesty hard to resist. Two types of Christians make very poor witnesses in their final days. First, there are those who stoically pretend that they are not suffering in any way. When Jesus was on the cross, he allowed people to see the agony he was in. His honesty allowed the thief on the cross to feel a kinship of suffering and made him open to receive salvation. Second, there are those who use their suffering as an excuse to be selfish or childish. If we become overly demanding of or neglectful in thanking those around us, few of them will think of us as a Christian.

Yes, we should be concerned about our unsaved loved ones. But God, who in his grace came into our lives, also has grace reserved for them. We may not live to see them accept it. It is one of those things which is entirely in his time. But, we can pray that our loved ones will at last to be able to sing with us:

> I once was lost but now am found,
> Was blind but now I see.
>
> —John Newton, 1725–1807
> "Amazing Grace"

We are hard pressed on every side, but not crushed; perplexed, but not in despair; persecuted, but not abandoned; struck down, but not destroyed. We always carry around in our body the death of Jesus, so that the life of Jesus may also be revealed in our body.

—2 Corinthians 4:8–10

Chapter 14

"MY BODY: MY BETRAYER OR MY FRIEND?"

*One of the Most Difficult Relationships We
Have Is with Our Own Body*

We are never so aware of how fragile our bodies really are until they start failing. Even with normal aging, our senses dim, almost as though our bodies are weakening our connection to this life in order to prepare us for the afterlife. Rage and depression can result.

And as we near death, we expect less service from our bodies. As one man explained it: "People ask how my brother is, and I say, 'Fine.' But 'fine' used to mean he was captain of the soccer team. . . . Now 'fine' means he didn't throw up today."

Still God graces our existence. If we cannot prepare food, we can still enjoy the taste. But if we cannot taste an apple pie, perhaps we can still enjoy the smell. If we are tired of being poked and prodded, perhaps we can still appreciate a hug, a gentle touch, a sweet massage. If we cannot bear the slightest touch, perhaps we can be soothed by the sweetest whisper, favorite music, children playing, or the sounds of the outdoors.

Even while dying, our bodies remain temples of the Holy Spirit, the Comforter who strengthens and encourages us. He

helps us recognize even the love of God in us and the love of
God around us.

What do we have to look forward to in our spiritual bodies?
Even here on earth there are sounds we humans cannot hear,
colors we cannot see, odors we cannot smell, and physical sen-
sations we cannot taste or feel. And, oh, the rich variety of what
we can perceive! Thousands of animals and thousands of plants
in the air, land, and water of just one small bit of the universe.
And on this one small planet he has showered a wealth of sur-
roundings for us—icy tundras, steamy jungles, rolling prairies,
daunting mountains, forests, beaches . . .

Since God has so richly dressed this temporary home, how
much more, then, has he provided for us in heaven?

> No eye has seen,
>   no ear has heard,
> no mind has conceived
>   what God has prepared for those who love him.
> (1 Corinthians 2:9; see also Isaiah 64:4)

As our body's abilities fade, we are compelled to face our
sense of identity. So often, our bodies keep us from looking at
ourselves—who we are really. Did we define ourselves by
gender? Now it is likely that sexuality is moot. Did we define
ourselves by physical acts like keeping house or being physi-
cally fit? Now, we are not able. Our intelligence? Perhaps now
pain, fatigue, or medicine muddle our thoughts.

Possessions? Status? Now, meaningless and helpless to prevent our death.

What about our own moral goodness? We are loving, kind,
and honest—or we are not. Through our lives we have failed
at being good, and we have succeeded. God already knows

which has won out. But salvation is ours by simply believing in Jesus, not by anything which we do ourselves. Thank God!

What is left? Who are we? We are people God loved before we were born. Nothing that has happened since has changed that. The Father doesn't look at what has happened to our bodies; he looks at what remains in our hearts. What he sees is what really matters.

When God told the prophet Samuel to anoint one of Jesse's sons as Israel's next king, the prophet thought for sure that Jesse's son Eliab was the chosen one. Yet God had not chosen Eliab or any of his six brothers. God had chosen the youngest son, David, considered so unlikely that his father had left him behind to tend sheep. God himself explained his choice as follows:

> The LORD does not look at the things man looks at. Man looks at the outward appearance, but the LORD looks at the heart. (1 Samuel 16:7)

Even as believers in Christ, we may not have considered or fully realized what God does see when he looks at us. He sees us clean and spotless, with wrongdoing forgiven and forgotten. He sees his Holy Spirit dwelling within us. He sees us as brothers and sisters of Christ. He sees us—and he loves us.

> The body that is sown is perishable, it is raised imperishable; it is sown in dishonor, it is raised in glory; it is sown in weakness, it is raised in power; it is sown a natural body, it is raised a spiritual body. (1 Corinthians 15:42–44)

A father to the fatherless,
a defender of widows,
is God in his holy dwelling.
God sets the lonely in families.

—Psalm 68:5–6

Chapter 15

Meeting the Needs of Our Family

*How Do We Care for Our Loved Ones and
Their Needs in Our Final Hours?*

As we face leaving them, our families remain uppermost in our minds. We wonder how they will handle our deaths. Will they be able to mourn and then move on? Will they feel betrayed by our leaving? How can we care for them while we need so much physical care ourselves? How will they meet medical bills?

Again, we are faced with knowing that only God can provide for them. And as much as we love them, God loves them more. Jesus assures us:

> Are not five sparrows sold for two pennies? Yet not one of them is forgotten by God. Indeed, the very hairs of your head are all numbered. Don't be afraid; you are worth more than many sparrows. (Luke 12:6–7)

Knowing that we are helpless to be part of their future, what can we do for them? We can give them ourselves now, and pray for them now.

In the fuss and attention over our illness, they can sometimes feel invisible, taken for granted. The husband of one dying woman stood by her throughout, looking for all the world like a tower of strength. Most of the time, in most ways, he was. Yet, he did say, "Just once I wish someone would ask how I was doing before asking how she is doing."

Knowing that they are torn by emotions, too, we can give them permission to mourn or be angry, to be tired or distracted, and, most importantly, to move on. Showing that we truly believe death is only a temporary separation can strengthen them. Praying for them can give them wisdom and perseverance and strength.

We can give them space and time to continue with their lives even while ours is ending. We can reinforce the knowledge that they are loved by us, by others, and by God.

As in all our dealings, being open and honest with them can be the most precious gift of all. This does not mean our deathbed is the place for burdening them with long-held secrets or information that would hurt them. It does mean that since one unpleasant surprise has already been dealt them in our diagnosis, we should try not to give them any more. Also, being open with them allows them to be open with us—to express their feelings and concerns instead of hiding them away where misunderstanding can sour their lives later.

Communication allows you and your family to choose together whatever action you may wish to take or whatever help you may want. For instance, a single mother with cancer found solace in writing letters to her only child, a daughter, to be opened on each of her daughter's birthdays until she turned eighteen. That idea appealed strongly to me (Diane), but in talking about it with my husband, I chose not to do it because it might not be received as a loving message but as a command, something guilt-inducing from beyond the grave.

Early on, a friend offered to coordinate volunteers to perform all the household tasks for my husband, from laundry to cleaning to cooking. It was a generous offer I thought would cheer and relieve him since he was working full-time and caring for our daughter, but he told me "no" in no uncertain terms. He needed our home to be his refuge, with our privacy interrupted as little as possible. That was how he renewed his own strength to get through—in quiet, performing the daily routine chores of life. To him the thought of people, even friends with the best of intentions, being in his home was disruptive and unsettling.

And so we thanked our friend for the offer, but declined. Some offers were gratefully accepted, however, like transportation to and from the hospital one hundred miles away. And, when I eventually came home to recuperate, we did allow our church family to provide one meal a day for a month.

Refusing a kind offer once does not mean you cannot change your mind. It may be best to say simply, "Not yet, thanks, but maybe later?" As with my husband, a refusal does not mean a spouse is denying the seriousness of the situation, only that other needs may be more important to him or her.

In sum, the key to meeting our family's needs may be to communicate as openly as possible, as often as possible, in a loving way even when arguing. Yes, arguing. I remember the first time David and I argued after the diagnosis; I almost jumped for joy because I felt I was being treated as a regular person, not as a breakable object that needed tending to.

Of course there are issues spouses may not be able or willing to discuss. In prayer, we can ask God for guidance and resolution, trusting that he will provide.

Children's understanding, wisdom, and strength should not be underestimated. There is a reason Jesus tells us to have the faith of a child! Talk with children in a way they can understand.

Details and medical jargon are not necessary. Many times, it is enough to say you are very sick, and the doctors are doing their best to help you get well.

Actions do speak louder than words. Like the mimics they are, children will often mirror our own reaction to the situation. If we appear desperate and fearful, they will feel that way, too. It is amazing at what a young age children can sniff out the truth. If we do not truly believe that God is with us, they will know. If we are only mouthing words, they will know, too.

They may ask if you will die from being sick. And you may, but you may not. It is in God's hands. But you can assure them that if you do die, it is not their fault, and it is not because you want to leave them. It is simply that everyone must die, but God takes care of us and will take care of them, too.

That may be especially important for teenagers, who may act out or withdraw. They may not confide in you, for whatever reason. But you can encourage them to talk with someone they trust here on earth and also to talk to God.

Are we helpless in meeting our family's needs right now? No, not anymore helpless than when we are healthy, really; we are just more aware of our limitations now than we may have been. As much as we try, we cannot protect our loved ones from all harm; they can't protect us, either. There is only One who can keep us safe, who has conquered even death. Therefore, we can share with our families that just as there is a time to mourn, there is a time to dance and that "weeping may remain for a night, but rejoicing comes in the morning" (Ps. 30:5).

Therefore, if anyone is in Christ, he is a new creation; the old has gone, the new has come! All this is from God, who reconciled us to himself through Christ and gave us the ministry of reconciliation.

—2 Corinthians 5:17–18

Chapter 16

WRAPPING UP
CONFLICTED RELATIONSHIPS

Reconciliation Is Desirable, but Is It Even Possible?

Are you still fighting with someone? Have you experienced so much turmoil in certain relationships that now you avoid your brother, sister, spouse, child, or former friend? As we struggle with serious illness and face our own mortality, we realize that we can no longer just sweep this broken glass under the carpet. We sense a personal urgency when we hear the apostle John's words:

> If anyone says, "I love God," yet hates his brother, he is a liar. For anyone who does not love his brother, whom he has seen, cannot love God, whom he has not seen. (1 John 4:20)

What are we to do? It would be easier if there were just one thing we had to forgive or to change. But we run into conflict every time we try to communicate; trouble is woven into the very texture of our relationship with her or him. We are not just arguing about something; instead, we are fighting over who we are when we are with her or him.

Remember the story of Jacob and Esau. These twin brothers were born in conflict, literally struggling within their mother's womb. It wasn't what they did to each other that caused their animosity; their very natures seemed to be in conflict. Both of these twins wanted the role of being first in the family. This was not something that could be shared; there was no compromise that could be reached. The fact that the other one was alive was enough to make him an enemy.

It may be hard to look beneath all the things that another person has done to us and realize that the underlying issues need to be healed. Understanding why we have not gotten along with this person may require us to search long and hard. Our deepest motivations may be in competition with the passion and life direction of that other person. The source of our difficulties may lie at the very core of our opposing personalities.

Now, the trick in this stage of your life is to realize that both you and that other person have come to the place where the conflict no longer matters. Can you, right now, grant that person the space to be who she feels she should be? You may be adamantly opposed to everything that person stands for; you may want to shake him and shout, "Grow up!" But what is to be gained by it? If you could wave a magic wand and instantly change that person to be a certain way, would you? Isn't that what we call "playing God?" God doesn't need you to win your competition with this person (if he ever did). Do you want to go to your grave saying, "I'm right and he's wrong," or do you want to be at peace?

For Jacob, this turning point came late one night while he was crossing the river Jabbok. A form grabbed him in the dark and wrestled with him until he thought he would die. His life-long hatred for his brother was thrashed about in that muddy stream, until at daybreak, the revelation came to him. All this time he had not been fighting with another man, but with God. Who was it that made him be born second? Not Esau, but God. Who had to win in order for things to be right? Not Jacob, but God. Jacob had spent his whole life fighting with his brother because he wanted what Esau had as the beloved firstborn child of his father. Now at Jabbok he came to see that all he had to do was relax and trust God, and God would give him what he needed. Humbled by this understanding, Jacob was ready to meet his brother and truly embrace him for the first time.

In the last days of his earthly life, Paul wrote:

> For I am already being poured out like a drink offering, and the time has come for my departure. (2 Timothy 4:6).

This final part of our lives is all about preparing our very souls as a gift upon God's altar. The relationships that we have allowed to be broken for years are a blemish upon that offering. It is important that we try to communicate with this person and offer our peace. This may involve saying that you no longer want to prove who is right or wrong and that you simply accept him as he is. You will need to say that you have made a choice to love and forgive, not because you want anything in return but simply because you want to be at peace with him. You need to show that you wish the best for him.

How will he respond? He may respond with suspicion about your motives or simply continue to ignore you. This is his choice; it does not change the need you have at this time to accept him as he is and to entrust your relationship with him to God's hands.

Sometimes reconciliation in the flesh is not possible. The person we are alienated from may be dead or missing. Writing a letter expressing our feelings and then placing it at her grave or some other significant spot may bring the closure we need. Prayerfully reconsidering our relationship and laying it before our loving Father will benefit us spiritually.

Sometimes, no matter how hard we try, we cannot bring ourselves to contact this person and take the steps needed for reconciliation. We may even be barred legally from seeing this person or know that the strain would be unwise for our physical or mental condition. God is a God of compassion and mercy. Sometimes all we can offer him is that we wish we wanted to do what is right. God's grace will meet even this half step, and God will, in his time, heal all things.

Part 3

PUTTING OUR AFFAIRS IN ORDER

This section provides practical resources for ensuring appropriate medical treatment, wrapping up financial concerns, and personalizing one's memorial service. Parts of this section are written in consultation with attorney K. Lawrence Kemp.

Abraham left everything he owned to Isaac.
But while he was still living, he gave gifts to
the sons of his concubines and sent them away
from his son Isaac to the land of the east.

—Genesis 25:5–6

Chapter 17

A TIME TO GIVE GIFTS

What Does It Mean to Put Our Affairs in Order?

As Abraham approached the end of his life, his family ties had become complicated, to say the least. After Sarah's death he had remarried, and it was not his desire, nor did it seem to be God's will, that anyone intrude upon the special role of Isaac in the patriarchal succession. By taking decisive action, he not only prevented a squabble over his possessions but also expressed his wishes about who should become clan leader.

We can assume from the text that Abraham in some formal way clearly stated his will that Isaac be his sole inheritor. Besides whatever monetary value this action had, there was great symbolic value to this legal act. Because Isaac did not have to prove his leadership role in the family, taking over the business went smoother than it would have otherwise.

Second, we read of Abraham's giving gifts to his other relatives. Since these were given while he was alive, he had the opportunity to tell recipients of his affection for them. In doing this he not only defused possible hard feelings but also prevented any objections to Isaac's becoming his sole beneficiary. Further, one can picture Abraham in his final weeks making use of his extensive friendships and political connections to ensure that his relatives would be successfully established in the east.

We can learn many things from Abraham's example. The first is that getting our affairs in order can be an act of faith. Our loved ones will remember the process as a sign of our sincerity and will appreciate our taking special time for them.

It is not always safe to assume that the obvious person will simply get everything when we die. Even if our intentions are as simple as "I want everything to go to my only living son, Isaac," there may be legal complications. When a person dies without a valid will, the intestate laws of the state govern the disposition of property; in apportioning property, these laws may assign more value to certain relationships than you do. Further, certain assets that you wanted to see remain intact may have to be sold and divided. If you have a will but it is out of date or poorly drawn, there may also be items not mentioned that will be handled in ways you would not wish.

How you leave your affairs delivers a message. If you simply leave matters for the courts to decide, then there may be delays in settling your estate, and your family members may be left confused about your wishes. Careful thought and timely revisions allow you to demonstrate the integrity with which you lived your life. Also, because you prayed about it, your possessions may have more influence for good than their material value would warrant.

There may be some gifts that you wish to distribute while you are living. As you give these gifts, you may want to say, "I give this to you now, not because I am close to dying but because you will have more opportunity to make use of this than I will." During a serious illness, many people want to simplify their lives. Even if we hope to recover, the spiritual effect of sickness is to reduce our grip on the material world. The fact that we do not care as much about certain things around the house may connect with the chance to make a friend or loved one happy and to express our feeling toward them.

Four rules need to be carefully followed:

1. *Give the person the opportunity to refuse the gift.* We may have a hard time imagining why a person would not take what we offer. Yet the person may not have an appropriate place in her home for the item. The item may require some form of care which she is unable to give. She also may have fears about what the other family members think. Refusing our gift does not mean she refuses our love or is not grateful; it simply means she is following her own wisdom about what is appropriate for the way she lives.

2. *Give with as few strings as possible.* A gift is not a gift if it comes with restrictions. Ask yourself, "Would I feel badly if the person receiving this item sold it, stored it, or used it differently than I would?" You must be prepared either to put aside any qualms you have or to discuss them openly with the person before presenting the gift. If you are not prepared to do this, then you may not be ready to give the gift.

3. *Do not give impulsively or in response to some influence a person is exerting on you.* Most of us have a loved one who is charming and persuasive. Then again, we also have dear ones who hint and nag until we give in to them. On a blue day, we might make an impulsive gift to brighten our spirits. Instead of building relationships of love and proving our faithful stewardship of God's blessings in our own life, gifts prompted by these types of circumstances can cause others to question our competence.

4. *Keep a list of each gift you give, to whom, when, and why you gave it.* This will save much heartache for your family after you are gone. Even if an item is of little monetary value, inevitably there will be someone who questions if you really intended for so-and-so to have it. You may wish to sign and date each item on the list the day that you give it and keep the original with your will while a second copy is kept where you can refer to it. This also helps prevent the embarrassing situation of giving the same item to two different people.

All of these issues are related to the important biblical concepts of stewardship. Stewardship involves carefully reflecting about all the material gifts God has given us and wisely perceiving that we are but trustees over these things. When we pass from this world, we have a final opportunity to use what we possess in a way that honors God.

In speaking about this very matter, Jesus says, "So if you have not been trustworthy in handling worldly wealth, who will trust you with true riches" (Luke 16:11)?

What we possess is placed in our hands for use in this world. Jesus teaches us to hold material things lightly because they, in themselves, do not benefit the soul. By making thoughtful plans for passing on these gifts to the next generation, we honor God's wisdom in loaning us these things for a while. We also find ourselves prayerfully depending upon God's guidance so that our giving can be a part of his grace for meeting the needs of others.

In those days Hezekiah became ill and was at the point of death. The prophet Isaiah son of Amoz went to him and said, "This is what the L<small>ORD</small> *says: Put your house in order, because you are going to die; you will not recover." Hezekiah turned his face to the wall and prayed to the* L<small>ORD</small>.

—2 Kings 20:1–2

Chapter 18

WHERE THERE'S
A WILL . . .

What Kind of Estate Planning Should We Do?

When people talk about "putting their affairs in order," they are not referring to just a few sentences that can be quickly uttered on their deathbeds. In fact, a number of decisions should not be made under the duress of impending death but rather should be made and adjusted throughout our lives. Whether we are in good health or ill, we should have a plan for our body, our remembrance, our possessions, our dependents, and our soul. It turned out that God granted Hezekiah a miraculous recovery; however, the prayerful ordering of his life did prove to be beneficial, and eventually his plans were put to use.

As Christians, we accept that life is both brief and uncertain. Making a will, completing an organ donation card, planning for our loved ones' care, and arranging for our funeral— all are actions responsible people take regardless of their health. There is nothing morbid about planning for the day we go to be with the Lord, and there is a great deal of wisdom in recognizing that only God knows when that day will be.

Further, wills and other arrangements should be adjusted as circumstances change in our lives. Changes in marital status, dependents, business partnerships, and the ownership of property can make previous documents obsolete. Having a spiritual renewal can also affect the way we feel about what we leave behind, prompting us to include charities, mission work, or our church in our will.

A *will* is a written document, signed in the presence of witnesses, that lays out our wishes for the dispersion of our possessions and the guardianship of our dependents. A will can be prepared or adjusted without a lawyer, but to do so may be penny-wise and pound-foolish. While many people today are turning to the Internet and popular books for "fill-in-the-blank-type" documents, estate laws vary significantly from state to state. A "boiler-plate" document may fail to deal with our individual circumstances. Wills also allow us to state our preference for who will care for our dependent minor children.

Your will is not the place to say hurtful things about people. You should be mindful of your Christian obligation to forgive, and very little good comes from such delayed expressions of anger. One option to consider is writing an explanatory letter to be read along with your will. This letter can be more in your personal style, explaining the choices you made and expressing your personal well wishes for all those you leave behind.

If you are leaving your house to someone, you may wish to consider setting up a *life estate*. This in effect transfers the property to that person while still permitting you full use of it while you are living. A life estate removes the property from the other items of your will and the probate process, avoiding certain fees. Life estates, as well as annuities and life insurance benefits, can be given directly to charities. For instance, if you live adjacent to a church, even if it is not your own, you may wish to inquire about their need for the building or for parking.

Probate is the normal process of officially presenting a will to the court. For this and the other matters of your estate, you will need to choose an executor or executrix (man or woman) to oversee your will, pay off any unpaid debts or bills, and close out your affairs. This person does not need legal or accounting expertise but should be someone you trust. Look for someone who knows you and your family well and who is responsible enough to ensure that even small matters such as canceling the newspaper are not overlooked. Besides writing checks and handling correspondence, this task will involve several days of running errands in your community and, possibly, selling property and possessions. You should ask people if they are willing to serve in this capacity. For handling this duty, the executor or executrix is allowed to charge a fee, based upon a percentage of your estate's worth.

You may also consider establishing a *trust* to provide for special concerns. If some of the recipients of your inheritance are minors or if you hope to encourage your grandchildren to go to college, you may leave money in a trust, which protects it until they reach a certain age or enter school. You may have a loved one who is a bit of the prodigal, and establishing a "spendthrift trust" will appoint a responsible party to dole out the sum gradually. Also, be aware that state laws will prevent you, as well they should, from making your inheritance coercive. In other words, you cannot require loved ones to marry or convert to another religion as a condition for receiving a gift. Common sense should guide all of your giving.

Besides reviewing your will, you also should check your life insurance and pension fund. Do they still name the people that you wish to be your beneficiaries? Some people do a lot of scheming with their estate in an attempt to avoid paying taxes or settling other commitments. This is perhaps to forget

that as Christians we have an obligation to pay taxes, as the
apostle Paul makes clear:

> Give everyone what you owe him: If you owe taxes,
> pay taxes; if revenue, then revenue; if respect, then re-
> spect; if honor, then honor. Let no debt remain out-
> standing, except the continuing debt to love one
> another, for he who loves his fellowman has fulfilled
> the law. (Romans 13:7–8)

Seeking to avoid taxes may also distract us from the primary consideration of estate planning, that is, ensuring that
those to whom we are leaving an inheritance receive what we
possess in a timely fashion. Consulting a person who is both
knowledgeable and trustworthy about financial planning may
not only prevent delays but also may allow a greater portion
of our assets to go to the people and charitable causes that we
care about. One option that you may wish to explore is called
a *charitable remainder trust.* In this we give stock, bonds, or other
assets to a charity with the stipulation that the interest go to a
loved one for as long as the person lives. This mechanism allows both our family members and our charities to benefit
from our estate.

It is surprising how many Christians fail to consider the
needs of the church or their favorite mission project in their
financial planning. While we are living, our tithes represent a
faithful stewardship to the Lord's work. After we are gone, a
gift from our estate can fund special needs beyond the normal church budget. Worthwhile projects, such as starting a
new teen outreach ministry or even getting the organ tuned,
may be waiting for memorial funds in your place of worship.
Since only God knows the future, it is important not to place

too many restrictions on your gift. Also, be aware that if you plan to give property to your church, the church governing body has to decide whether the church can use the property.

In summary, as you put your financial affairs in order:

- Pray, trusting that God will provide you with wisdom.
- Choose appropriate legal counsel as well as a trustworthy person to act as executor.
- Provide for your loved ones thoughtfully.
- Give with your heart to the charities you love.

Now we know that if the earthly tent we live in is destroyed, we have a building from God, an eternal house in heaven, not built by human hands. Meanwhile we groan, longing to be clothed with our heavenly dwelling. . . . We do not wish to be unclothed but to be clothed with our heavenly dwelling, so that what is mortal may be swallowed up by life.

—2 Corinthians 5:1–5

Chapter 19

CARING FOR THE BODY

Living Wills, Organ Donor Forms, and Powers of Attorney:
What Do They All Mean?

P aul uses two images to talk about how the physical body relates to the soul. He calls the body a tent that will one day be folded up and exchanged for a heavenly home, and, in a similar fashion, he describes the body as only clothing for the soul. Both of these images are comforting thoughts as we struggle through an illness that diminishes our earthly frame. Remember, God has designed our bodies to last for just a short time. Like threadbare clothing, our bodies are eventually discarded, and we will leave this tent behind, confident that God has provided a permanent home in heaven.

Paul's words can also serve to guide us through the four decisions we need to make about our physical body. Two of those decisions deal with how we wish others to respond if our bodies or our minds deteriorate further before we die. The other two are directions that we leave in order to guide those responsible for our body after our deaths. Failure to make these decisions ourselves may unnecessarily burden our families or leave strangers in charge of our affairs.

Knowing that God designed the body to house us only for a time, we may want to leave instructions to prevent heroic or unnatural efforts being made to keep us in the body. An *advance directive*, or *living will*, is a legal document indicating the extent to which we wish medical treatment to be administered to keep us alive. In it we list the treatments we do not wish to receive, providing that we are not conscious to express our wishes at the time. This list may be altered at any time and may include:

- an order not to perform cardiac resuscitation (CPR)
- a request not to be placed on a ventilator (mechanical respiration)
- a request not to be given a feeding tube or other invasive form of nutrition
- a request not to be given intravenous fluids
- a request not to be given blood products or blood
- a denial of permission for further surgery or invasive tests
- a request not to receive kidney dialysis
- a request not to be given antibiotics

All Christians have to come to a personal decision about what they consider to be an appropriate use of medical technology for their circumstance. Each of the above medical procedures has successfully helped people return to health and enjoy years of life. If, however, the body is beyond its capacity to return to conscious life, these procedures may support a prolonged vegetative state or coma. The personal choices we make in this document reflect our own optimism about recovery from setbacks caused by our illness as well as our thoughts regarding the extent of the measures that physicians should take to preserve life.

A fill-in-the-blank *advance directive* form may be obtained from most healthcare providers, on the Internet, or from your lawyer. This form should be signed and dated in the presence of two witnesses (some states vary here and may require notarization). You will also need to choose an agent, that is, a person who knows you well and who can assist in making decisions about your health care if you are unconscious. This person needs to be someone you can trust to make your wishes known. Once completed and signed, your advance care directive should be photocopied and given to your primary care physician and your agent. The original should be kept in an accessible secure place (not in your safety deposit box).

The second issue we need to consider has to do with our mental dependability. If we have periods when our thinking is fuzzy or if we can no longer trust our memory, we may need to choose a dependable person to handle our finances. Although our soul is spiritual and eternal and therefore is not affected by the loss of blood flow to our brains, our minds are a different story. They belong to our frail, earthly body. There is no shame in recognizing this fact and preparing a suitable person to act in our place.

A *power of attorney* is a legal document that entrusts a person we name with control over some or all of our money-related issues. Here again, it is important that this person be someone that we trust and that the actual document be specific as to what powers we are granting. You may limit your power of attorney to be only responsible for particular aspects of your affairs, such as your checking account. You may also limit when the power of attorney is in effect, so that the person you choose takes over when you are hospitalized or otherwise incapacitated, but the document is revoked if you recover.

Having a suitable power of attorney avoids the potential heartbreak of your family's having to prove that you are incompetent to the courts.

After we have gone to be with the Lord, what to do with our bodies presents another set of decisions. While our bodies, as a whole, may no longer serve our purposes and be sloughed off like an old set of clothes, certain parts of our bodies may provide much needed organ and tissue transplants for others. Many Christians consider this to be a matter of faithful stewardship. If I knew someone else could use a good suit, I wouldn't throw it in the trash; in the same way, I would like to provide doctors with the opportunity to harvest any usable organs when I have gone beyond this body. Here again, a *universal organ donor* form can be obtained from your physician, and you will be able to set limits on how your body is to be used, if you desire.

Finally, we need to leave instructions about whether we wish our bodies to be cremated or interred whole. While we are aware of no Scripture passages that argue against cremation, there are still a few ethnic groups and Christian denominations that discourage the practice. For most Christians this decision seems to be purely a matter of personal choice and cultural heritage. Cremation does not in any way prevent you from having a viewing or a full funeral service.

In summary, as you make decisions about your earthly body:

- Pray, trusting that God will provide you with wisdom.
- Provide the advance directive (living will), which speaks your wishes, and choose an appropriate person to act as agent.

- If you are concerned about your diminished mental state, choose someone to handle your financial affairs.
- Decide if you wish to be an organ donor.
- Choose how you wish your remains to be returned to earth.

I have fought the good fight, I have finished the race, I have kept the faith.

—2 Timothy 4:7

Chapter 20

ONE FAIR FAREWELL

How Do We Want to Be Remembered?

How do we let people say good-bye to us? How do we witness, one final time, to our faith in the resurrection and our heavenly home? How do we say "See you later!" to those who will catch up again with us someday in heaven? Funerals are not necessary evils but rather meaningful expressions of faith, hope, and love in the face of death. They speak of spiritual connections that death cannot sever.

As a service of worship, your funeral will do four things:

1. It will say thank you to God for the gift of your life.
2. It will remind those present of God's promises concerning eternal life.
3. It will remind those who are unsure of their faith of their mortality.
4. It will provide a special time for the comfort of the Holy Spirit to minister to those who grieve your passing.

Leaving some form of directions for your funeral gives you a chance to share something of your own experience of the gospel with those gathered. Many Christians assume that leaving it to the minister is best because they are the experts, but that clergyperson will not know your family and friends the way you do. Those who come to your farewell will want to hear your words or at least something that you choose to have read. The minister can change and improve on your plans, adding whatever is needed to make the service complete, but your contribution will likely be what is remembered.

The first choice you must make is whether the service should be held in your church, the funeral home, or elsewhere. As a pastor, I (Bill) encourage even non-attending Christians to make use of a church facility if at all possible. People no longer see a church funeral as a statement about your importance to that church but rather as an opportunity to be with others who loved you and to see death in a religious context. Not only does a church setting provide more flexibility in the use of hymns and musical instruments, it also visually reinforces the connection between your personal faith and the faith of a community that celebrates Jesus' resurrection every Easter.

You will also need to decide about viewing or visitation. There seems to be a basic human need for family members and friends to comfort each other and gather for conversation both before and after the service. The "viewing" is not so much about people coming to look at you as it is about providing a chance for all those who knew you to interact with your family members and each other. I have noticed that this process seems to go about the same, whether there is a body present or simply photographs on display. If you are uncomfortable about being viewed or if you wish to have an immediate cremation, you can still request visitation times at which a photograph display and flower arrangement will serve well in your stead.

In planning for your funeral, you are not expected to outline the entire order of worship. What will personalize your service is a short list of favorite Scripture passages, hymns, poems, or quotations you wish others to hear. Along with these selections you may want to note why you chose them or even offer a few thoughts of your own. If the music you have chosen is not available, the clergyperson may still choose to read the verses and note how they were significant to your life. If the person officiating is unlikely to know you well, you may wish to ask a friend or family member if he or she would be willing to prepare a short eulogy.

Some favorite hymns appropriate for funerals are:

- "Abide with Me"
- "Amazing Grace"
- "Be Still My Soul"
- "Blessed Assurance"
- "Christ the Lord Is Risen Today"
- "For All the Saints"
- "How Great Thou Art"
- "I'll Fly Away"
- "In the Garden"
- "It Is Well with My Soul"
- "The Old Rugged Cross (On a Hill Far Away)"
- "The Strife Is O'er"
- "What a Friend We Have in Jesus"
- "When the Roll Is Called Up Yonder"

Note that a song does not need to be about death to be a part of the service. Some people request very lively songs with the hope that others will sense their joy in reaching heaven. If you are considering a secular song, however, you may wish to consult with your pastor to see if the church has a policy against such music.

Some frequently cited Scripture passages include the following:

- Psalm 23: The Shepherd's Psalm
- Ecclesiastes 3:1–13: "There is a time for everything . . ."
- Isaiah 40:28–31: "They will soar on wings like eagles . . ."
- John 11:17–27: "I am the resurrection . . ."
- John 14:1–6: "In my Father's house are many rooms . . ."
- Romans 8:28–39: "All things God works together for the good of those who love him . . ."
- 1 Corinthians 13: The Love Chapter
- 1 Corinthians 15: "Christ . . . the firstfruits of those who have fallen asleep."
- 2 Corinthians 4:16–5:3: "Our heavenly dwelling . . ."
- 1 Thessalonians 4:13–18: "Meeting the Lord in the Air"
- 2 Timothy 4:6–8: "I have fought the good fight . . ."
- Revelation 21:1–7: "Then I saw a new heaven and a new earth . . ."

Finally, do not place your funeral plans in your safety deposit box; leave them in a location that is easily found and accessible. Share these plans with your pastor, and let your family know where you have placed your copy. You may also wish to make prearrangements with a funeral director. Your spouse or children may not be willing or able to discuss your service with you, but if you take the initiative, you will find someone who will see that your wishes are respected.

In summary, as you plan your farewell:

- Pray that God may be honored and praised in this service of worship.
- Choose Scripture passages and hymns that witness of your faith experience.
- Provide a few notes about why you have made these choices.
- Think of how you want to be remembered.

Part 4

COMMITTING OURSELVES TO GOD

This section contains final words and thoughts for the heaven-bound soul.

*Examine yourselves to see whether you are in
the faith; test yourselves.*

—2 Corinthians 13:5

Chapter 21

Ready or Not for God

Belief, Repentance, and Rest:
How Do We Walk These Final Steps in Our Journey?

With outstretched arms, God waits to welcome us. Are we ready spiritually? Preparing ourselves to meet God face to face is the one part of dying that is ours alone. No one else can do it for us.

There are only three steps in the soul's final journey—believe, repent, and rest. They are precious and important steps. You may already believe that God loves you and sent his only son to pay the price for all of mankind's sins. You know that our loving Father is not willing to let even one person die estranged from him.

If you are unsure about your faith, today is the day to simply believe. While there are no certain words to pray, many people have been helped by reciting the following simple prayer, commonly called the Sinner's Prayer.

Dear Lord Jesus,

I know I am a sinner. I believe you died for my sins. Right now, I turn from my sins and open the door of my heart and life. I receive you as my personal Lord and Savior. Thank you for saving me. Amen.

If you are unsure about God's forgiveness, today is the day to simply repent. As we look back on our lives, we may be prompted to apologize to God for wrongdoing. He himself has given us a guide to help us look at various areas of our lives, a guide called the Ten Commandments. And while Jesus brought new understanding of our God as a loving Father, the laws given to Moses are useful as a sort of checklist. As given in the book of Exodus, chapter 20, the first four commandments deal with our relationship with God; the rest deal with our relationships with other people.

In our relationship with God, we are to have only one God. We are not to worship idols—this means not just statues but also earthly things like money or power. We are not to use God's name without reverence. This does not mean swearing; it means denying God. We are to keep one day in seven as a day devoted to honoring God and to rest.

In our dealings with others, we are to respect our parents and family. We are to preserve life. We are to remain faithful to our spouse. We are to respect other's property. We are to tell the truth. We are to be content with our own possessions.

At one time or another, all of us have fallen short of these commands, but God makes a simple way to put things right. We just tell him we know we have done wrong, that we are sorry, and that we will try to do better. King David was called a man after God's own heart (Acts 13:22) not because he always did right but because when he realized he did wrong, he was truly sorry and told God so. The Psalms are proof of that.

This was the most liberating spiritual lesson I (Diane) learned during my first bout with cancer. I was so angry. I purposely tried to provoke my pastor when he came to visit. I raged and railed. At the age of thirty-two, with a long-awaited only child just a year old, I had stage IV cancer. Even if I eventually recovered, a hysterectomy meant I could never have another child. It also meant a very early menopause and, in my mind, a shorter life.

When the pastor entered my room, I looked him square in the face and said, "I am pissed off at God, and I told him so."

He answered, "Go ahead. He's big enough to take it. Just keep talking to him."

What relief his advice gave then and continues to give now. God gave us our emotions, and he already knows what we are feeling whether we tell him or not. So we can tell him all, knowing that he understands and will help us, if we are sincere.

Are you still unsettled? Today is the day to simply trust and rest in God's love, knowing he more than returns our love and forgives us all.

As Jesus said:

> Come to me, all you who are weary and burdened, and I will give you rest. Take my yoke upon you and learn from me, for I am gentle and humble in heart, and you will find rest for your souls. (Matthew 11:28–29)

The disciple John described the message of God's forgiveness:

> God is light; in him there is no darkness at all. . . . If we claim to be without sin, we deceive ourselves and the truth is not in us. If we confess our sins, he is faithful and just and will forgive us our sins and purify us from all unrighteousness. (1 John 1:5, 8–9)

God doesn't say, "Well, I forgive all those little wrongs, but when you get here, we'll have to discuss those big sins." No, he forgives all.

Now we can rest, happily expecting eternity despite remembering our failures, for as the prophet wrote:

> I remember my affliction and my wandering,
>   the bitterness and the gall.
> I well remember them,
>   and my soul is downcast within me.
> Yet this I call to mind
>   and therefore I have hope:
>
> Because of the LORD's great love we are not consumed,
>   for his compassions never fail.
> They are new every morning;
>   great is your faithfulness.
> I say to myself, "The LORD is my portion;
>   therefore I will wait for him."
>
> The LORD is good to those whose hope is in him,
>   to the one who seeks him;
> it is good to wait quietly
>   for the salvation of the LORD.
>   —Lamentations 3:19–26

So now, loved one, wait. Wait, and rest.

Jesus took bread, gave thanks and broke it. . . .
Then he took the cup, gave thanks and
offered it.

—Mark 14:22–23

Chapter 22

THANKS FOR THE GIFT

Reflecting on the Various Aspects of a Full Life:
How Do We Say Thank You to God?

Jesus saw the approach of his own death as an occasion for giving thanks. In fact, the liturgical word *eucharist* comes from the Greek word for giving thanks. What could Jesus possibly be giving thanks for?

Not for the pain that he would face in death. It is only human that we find that pain and discomfort rob us of a thankful attitude.

Not for the fact that his disciples would desert him. In our final days, we struggle to keep thankful when we are lonely.

Not for the difficulty he would have carrying his cross to his execution. Some days each task becomes a burden, and we find it hard to say thank you to God.

And yet there is something mysterious and divine in the midst of his suffering that kept Jesus able to remain thankful. His heart sorrowed to know that he would be parted from his friends, and yet he was thankful for their friendship. He felt the nails, the crown of thorns, the agony, and yet he was thankful to be the savior of the world. He felt the weight of sin, and yet he was thankful to lift the cup of his blood and offer forgiveness to all. Can this same victorious spirit of thanksgiving reign in our hearts today? Yes!

On his final evening Jesus also said, "I tell you the truth, anyone who has faith in me will do what I have been doing" (John 14:12).

Being thankful in the midst of death was one of the things he was confident his friends would be able to do, because they would receive his Spirit. This comforting and supporting Holy Spirit is available to us and is made evident to others by our thankfulness.

But what could Jesus, or we, be thankful for?

Just like us, Jesus was thankful for being given the gift of life, even though it was short. Because he lived on earth, he felt the nurturing love of his mother, the embrace of his friends, and the joy of those who appreciated his touch. Being in the flesh brought pain, but it also brought the fullness of the human experience. What would we have missed if we had never been born?

One of the most memorable and popular films of all time is Jimmy Stewart's *It's a Wonderful Life*. It shows how many people are affected by one life and how rarely we notice the good we bring to others as we live. It also shows how the distress of this moment can hide from our eyes a lifetime of experiences for which we should be thankful.

For people of faith, thankfulness is not something that is supposed to arise because our lives are long, perfect, and full of good things; thankfulness is in our hearts because we have had life. However short or difficult that gift has been, we are thankful because God could have chosen not to give that gift to us at all.

Remember Job? The Devil comes into heaven one day and challenges God by saying that the only reason that Job is thankful and praises God is because his life has been filled with good things. God had indeed gifted Job with good things, and when God took away family, wealth, and, finally, Job's health, Job did find it hard to be thankful. Like Jimmy Stewart's character in the previously mentioned movie, he began to be sorry he had ever been born. When Job's wife came to him and said, "Why don't you curse God and die," Job turned on her and asked, "Shall we accept good from God, and not trouble?" (Job 3:10). Throughout his long illness Job's heart carried a small kernel of faith and thanksgiving for life itself. The one point that defeated the Devil's argument was that it is possible for a person to praise God, even when he is suffering.

As Job expressed in his worship, we come into this world with nothing, and no matter what we experience through life or gain from this world, we return naked (Job 1:21). The end of life is a stripping-away process. We lose our health, then all of the money we accumulated seems to go to doctors and medicines, and finally we are stripped away even from our loved ones, but nevertheless, God is to be praised. The gift of life becomes even more awe-inspiring to us as we prepare to give it back to the one who gave it to us for a time.

In 1637, after a year of such sickness and hardship that he had buried five thousand from his town, the Lutheran pastor Martin Rinkart expressed his praise for God with these words:

> Now thank we all our God,
>   with hearts and hands and voices.
> Who wondrous things has done,
>   in whom this world rejoices.
> Who from our mother's arms
>   has blessed us on our way
> With countless gifts of love,
>   and still is ours today.
>   —"Now Thank We All Our God"

In the same way, the Spirit helps us in our weakness. We do not know what we ought to pray for, but the Spirit himself intercedes for us with groans that words cannot express. And he who searches our hearts knows the mind of the Spirit, because the Spirit intercedes for the saints in accordance with God's will.

—Romans 8:26–27

Chapter 23

SIMPLE PRAYERS

Helps for Praying when We Don't Feel Like Saying Much

Through the Holy Spirit, God makes it easy for us to talk to him, no matter the circumstance. Praying is simply that, conversing with him. When we pray, it doesn't matter where we are, what position we are in, or how many words we use. Sometimes, we don't need words at all.

Prayer without words? Yes! Tears, laughter, embraces, moans, giggles, smiles, and songs can all be expressions of the soul within us as we seek communion with God. The Holy Spirit takes the intent of our hearts when we pray, rephrases that intent, and makes it pleasing to God and in accordance with his will. Therefore, if we are sincere, we don't need to worry about whether a prayer is "right."

One-word prayers can speak volumes. Simple words like "Thanks," "Please," "Help," "Come," " Peace," " Yes," "Okay," "Amen." So can simple phrases like "Lord, have mercy"; "I rest my soul in thee"; "Thy will be done"; "I am yours"; "Jesus, remember me"; "Alleluia, amen."

If it is not God who needs the words, then it must be us. Maybe the words clarify our thinking or help us concentrate on communicating with our Father. For instance, one Christian made it a habit to pull an empty chair up near her bed and imagined God sitting there as she told him of her day.

Like Tevye in *Fiddler on the Roof,* we are to be in constant communication with God, praying "without ceasing." We can be spontaneous in our prayer, speaking the way we would talk to a dear friend.

Sometimes, though, we struggle through confusion, fear, fatigue, or even happiness to find words. That is when the prayers passed down from believer to believer through generations can help. There are prayers that have been prayed by millions of people as they have gathered for worship. As individual Christians, we can use the same prayers when we worship in private.

Both reciting prayers passed down through generations and prayers in words rising from our hearts have a place in a believer's life.

Is prayer still important and effective in our final hours? Yes. Just before he was arrested in Gethsemane, Jesus prayed for himself, for his disciples, and, then, for you and me:

> I pray also for those who will believe in me through their [the disciples'] message, that all of them may be one, Father, just as you are in me and I am in you. May they also be in us so that the world may believe that you have sent me. I have given them the glory that you gave me, that they may be one as we are one: I in them and you in me. May they be brought to complete unity to let the world know that you sent me and have loved them even as you have loved me. (John 17:20–23)

Below are some traditional prayers you may wish to use during your own times of personal prayer. We begin with the Lord's Prayer, which is the example Jesus gave to his disciples when they asked how they ought to pray.

The Lord's Prayer

Our Father in heaven,
hallowed be your name,
your kingdom come,
your will be done
on earth as it is in heaven.
Give us today our daily bread.
Forgive us our debts,
as we also have forgiven our debtors.
And lead us not into temptation,
but deliver us from the evil one.

—Matthew 6:9–13

Note: the line in which we request forgiveness for our sins can also be read "forgive us our trespasses as we forgive those who trespass against us" or "forgive us our sins as we forgive those who sin against us." At the end of the prayer, some churches add the line: "For thine is the kingdom and the power and the glory, forever."

The next two are prayers of praise and thanksgiving to God, which may also be prayed in song:

Doxology

Praise God from whom all blessings flow;
Praise Him, all creatures here below;
Praise Him above, ye heavenly host;
Praise Father, Son, and Holy Ghost. Amen

Glory Be to the Father

Glory be to the Father, and to the Son, and to the Holy Ghost; as it was in the beginning, is now, and ever shall be. World without end. Amen.

The next two prayers are useful in confessing our sins and preparing ourselves to receive God's mercy. The Scripture passages that follow them are God's words of assurance to us that we have been forgiven. You should pray the prayer of confession, pause, and then read the words of assurance.

A Modern Prayer of Confession

Dear God,

You see all that I have done—good things and bad things, secret things and show-off things. You know my words and thoughts, both kind and unkind. Even more, you see the good I have failed to do and the bad I have wished on others.

There is much which I am sorry for and ashamed of. There is little to offer in my defense.

Here I fall fully on your mercy as one who loves me. Please clothe the feeble offering of my life in your grace. Let your Son's perfect offering of himself be my resting place. Please heal my soul with your perfect love and, through the Holy Spirit, grant me comfort and peace.

I will try not to cause you pain again, yet I know that I will fail. I also know that you love me and promise to forgive me. For that, dear God, I thank you. I recommit myself, in my remaining days to love others, as you have called me to do, through the grace of Jesus my Lord and Savior. Amen.

Words of Assurance

If we claim to be without sin, we deceive ourselves and the truth is not in us. If we confess our sins, he is faithful and just and will forgive us our sins and purify us from all unrighteousness. (1 John 1:8–9)

David's Confession in Psalm 51:1–10

Have mercy on me, O God,
   according to your unfailing love;
according to your great compassion
   blot out my transgressions.
Wash away all my iniquity
   and cleanse me from my sin.

For I know my transgressions,
   and my sin is always before me.
Against you, you only, have I sinned
   and done what is evil in your sight,
so that you are proved right when you speak
   and justified when you judge.
Surely I was sinful at birth,
   sinful from the time my mother conceived me.
Surely you desire truth in the inner parts;
   you teach me wisdom in the inmost place.

Cleanse me with hyssop, and I will be clean;
   wash me, and I will be whiter than snow.
Let me hear joy and gladness;
   let the bones you have crushed rejoice.
Hide your face from my sins
   and blot out all my iniquity.

Create in me a pure heart, O God,
   and renew a steadfast spirit within me. Amen.

Words of Assurance

The sacrifices of God are a broken spirit;
    a broken and contrite heart,
    O God, you will not despise.

—Psalm 51:17

Psalm 103:8–14

The LORD is compassionate and gracious,
    slow to anger, abounding in love.
He will not always accuse,
    nor will he harbor his anger forever;
he does not treat us as our sins deserve
    or repay us according to our iniquities.
For as high as the heavens are above the earth,
    so great is his love for those who fear him;
as far as the east is from the west,
    so far has he removed our transgressions from us.
As a father has compassion on his children,
    so the LORD has compassion on those who fear him;
for he knows how we are formed,
    he remembers that we are dust.

The next two prayers are for spiritual and physical healing.

An Intercession

Almighty God,
    We pray that _____ (place your name here)
    may be comforted in their suffering and made whole.
    When they are afraid, give them courage;
    when they feel weak, grant them your strength;
    when they are afflicted, afford them patience;
    when they are lost, offer them hope;

when they are alone, draw near to them;
when death comes, open your arms to receive him/her.
In the name of Jesus Christ we pray. Amen.[1]

The Serenity Prayer

God, grant me the serenity to accept the things I cannot change,
the courage to change the things I can,
and the wisdom to know the difference. Amen

This last prayer is for becoming a Christian or rededicating your life to God:

The Sinner's Prayer

Dear Lord Jesus,

I know I am a sinner. I believe you died for my sins. Right now, I turn from my sins and open the door of my heart and life. I receive you as my personal Lord and Savior. Thank you for saving me. Amen.

Praise be to the God and Father of our Lord Jesus Christ, the Father of compassion and the God of all comfort, who comforts us in all our troubles, so that we can comfort those in any trouble with the comfort we ourselves have received from God.

—2 Corinthians 1:3–4

Chapter 24

FINAL WORDS

Comforting Thoughts from Others on Their Journey Home

God gives to some people the gift of creative writing and inspiring speech. When we search for words to express our feelings about going to be with the Lord, their words may suit our needs. They comfort us and may comfort our loved ones by reassuring them, too.

The Chariot

BECAUSE I could not stop for Death,
   He kindly stopped for me;
The carriage held but just ourselves
   And Immortality.

We slowly drove, he knew no haste,
   And I had put away
My labor, and my leisure too,
   For his civility.

We passed the school where children played,
   Their lessons scarcely done;
We passed the fields of gazing grain,
   We passed the setting sun.

We paused before a house that seemed
    A swelling of the ground;
The roof was scarcely visible,
    The cornice but a mound.

Since then 'tis centuries; but each
    Feels shorter than the day
I first surmised the horses' heads
    Were toward eternity.[1]

—Emily Dickinson

Prayer of an Injured Civil War Soldier

I asked God for strength, that I might achieve,
I was made weak that I might learn to humbly obey.

I asked for health that I might do great things,
I was given infirmity that I might do better things.

I asked for riches that I might be happy,
I was given poverty that I might be wise.

I asked for power, that I might have the praise of men,
I was given weakness that I might feel the need of God.

I asked for all things that I might enjoy life,
I was given life that I might enjoy all things.

I got nothing that I asked for, but everything that I had hoped for,
my prayer was answered. I am among all men, most richly
    blessed.

—Anonymous

Crossing the Bar

Sunset and evening star,
    And one clear call for me!
And may there be no moaning of the bar,
    When I put out to sea,

But such a tide as moving seems asleep,
    Too full for sound and foam,
When that which drew from out the boundless deep
    Turns again home.

Twilight and evening bell,
    And after that the dark!
And may there be no sadness of farewell,
    When I embark;

For tho' from out our bourne of Time and Place
    The flood may bear me far,
I hope to see my Pilot face to face
    When I have crost the bar.[2]

—Alfred Lord Tennyson

For Olivia Susan Clemens

The following epitaph was written by Mark Twain for his daughter, who died at age twenty-four on August 18, 1896.

Warm summer sun, shine kindly here;
Warm southern wind, blow softly here;
Green sod above, lie light, lie light.
Good night, dear heart, good night.[3]

There is a special sincerity and brevity to be found in the words that people of faith have spoken in the time close to their death.

John Wesley
Homecoming: March 2, 1791

After they rose from prayer [Wesley] took Mr. Broadbent's hand, drew him near, and with the utmost placidness saluted him, and said, *"Farewell, farewell."* He thus took leave of all who were in the room. When some one entered, he strove to speak. Finding that his friends could not understand what he said, he paused, and with all his remaining strength, cried out,

"The best of all is, God is with us."

Then, lifting up his dying arm in token of victory, and raising his feeble voice with a holy triumph not to be expressed, he again repeated the heart reviving words,

"The best of all is, God is with us."[4]

—John Telford

John Bunyan
Homecoming: 1688

I see myself now at the end of my journey: my toilsome days are ended. I am going to see that head which was crowned with thorns, and that face which was spit upon for me. I have formerly lived by hearsay and faith; but now I go where I shall live by sight, and shall be with Him in whose company I delight myself. I have loved to hear my Lord spoken of: and wherever I have seen the print of his shoe in the earth, there I have coveted to set my foot too.[5]

—John Bunyan
The Pilgrim's Progress

Rev. Henry Francis Lyte
Homecoming: November 20, 1847

Abide with me, fast falls the eventide;
The darkness deepens; Lord with me abide.
When other helpers fail, and comforts flee,
Help of the helpless, O abide with me.

—"Abide with Me"

In his final weeks, Henry Francis Lyte penned this simple poem. His evening meditations led him to reflect on how the two disciples who met Jesus on Easter eve implored him:

Stay with us, for it is nearly evening; the day is almost over. (Luke 24:29)

Our souls, as we are going home, crave contact with our Lord. It is natural for us to desire that the moments of spiritual peace that our meditations provide for us would remain with us through the lonely and painful times. We also wish for God to be gentle with us, for even now, the strength of our faith ebbs and flows. Experiencing this need for mercy, Lyte also wrote this verse, which is rarely sung with the hymn:

Come not in terrors as the King of kings,
but kind and good, with healing in thy wings,

tears for all woes, a heart for every plea,—
come, Friend of sinners, and thus abide with me.

—"Abide with Me"

The Apostle Paul
Homecoming: About A.D. 68

For I am already being poured out like a drink offering, and the time has come for my departure. I have fought the good fight, I have finished the race, I have kept the faith. Now there is in store for me the crown of righteousness, which the Lord, the righteous Judge, will award to me on that day—and not only to me, but also to all who have longed for his appearing. (2 Timothy 4:6–8)

Jesus
Homecoming: About A.D. 30

My God, my God, why have you forsaken me? (Matthew 27:46; Mark 15:34)

Father, forgive them; for they know not what they do. (Luke 23:34 KJV)

Today you will be with me in paradise. (Luke 23:43)

Father, into your hands I commit my spirit. (Luke 23:46)

Dear woman, here is your son. (John 19:26)

I am thirsty. (John 19:28)

It is finished. (John 19:30)

ENDNOTES

Chapter 5: Expect Loneliness

1. Daniel P. Sulmasy, M.D., Ph.D. and Maike Rahn, M.S., "I Was Sick and You Came to Visit Me: Time Spent at the Bedsides of Seriously Ill Patients with Poor Prognoses," *The American Journal of Medicine* 111, no. 5, (1 October 2001): 385–89.

Chapter 8: Forgiven and Forgiving

1. Thomas Fuller, in *The New Book of Christian Quotations*, comp. Tony Castle (New York: Crossroad Publishing Company, 1983), 89.

Chapter 10: If

1. Martin Luther King Jr., "The Three Dimensions of a Complete Life," a sermon delivered at New Covenant Baptist Church, Chicago, Illinois, on 9 April 1967.

Chapter 11: Different Strokes for Different Folks

1. Mitch Albom, *Tuesdays with Morrie* (Rockland, Mass.: Wheeler Pub., 1998).

Chapter 23: Simple Prayers

1. From "A Service of Healing," in *United Methodist Church Book of Worship* (Nashville, Tenn.: United Methodist Publishing House, 1992), 621.

Chapter 24: Final Words

1. Emily Dickinson, "The Chariot," in *Favorite Poems of Emily Dickinson*, ed. Mabel Loomis Todd and T. W. Higginson (1890; reprint, New York: Avenel Books, 1978), 138–39.

2. *The Poetic and Dramatic Works of Alfred Lord Tennyson*, Cambridge Edition (Boston and New York: Houghton Mifflin Company, 1898), 753.

3. The tombstone of Olivia Susan Clemens, to be found at Woodlawn Cemetery in Elmira, New York. Twain adapted the following popular poem of the time:

> Warm summer sun, shine friendly here;
> Warm western wind, blow kindly here;
> Green sod above, rest light, rest light—
> Good-night Annette! Sweetheart, good-night.
> —Robert Richardson (1850–1901)
> "To Annette"

4. John Telford, *The Life of John Wesley* (New York, Eaton & Mains; Cincinnati, Curts & Jennings, 1898), 350.

5. John Bunyan, *Pilgrim's Progress*, Element Classics of World Spirituality (Rockport, Mass.: Element Books, 1997), 310–11.